Narrative
Counseling
in Schools

Practical Skills for Counselors
Jeffrey A. Kottler, Series Editor

Narrative Counseling in Schools: Powerful & Brief
John Winslade, Gerald Monk

Helping in the Hallways: Advanced Strategies for Enhancing School Relationships
Richard J. Hazler

Brief Counseling That Works: A Solution-Focused Approach for School Counselors
Gerald B. Sklare

Deciphering the Diagnostic Codes: A Guide for School Counselors
W. Paul Jones

Success With Challenging Students
Jeffrey A. Kottler

John Winslade • Gerald Monk

Narrative Counseling in Schools

Powerful & Brief

CORWIN PRESS, INC.
A Sage Publications Company
Thousand Oaks, California

For information:

Corwin Press, Inc.
A Sage Publications Company
2455 Teller Road
Thousand Oaks, California 91320
E-mail: order@corwinpress.com

SAGE Publications Ltd.
6 Bonhill Street
London EC2A 4PU
United Kingdom

SAGE Publications India Pvt. Ltd.
M-32 Market
Greater Kailash I
New Delhi 110 048 India

Printed in the United States of America

Library of Congress Cataloging-in-Publication Data

Winslade, John.
    Narrative counseling in schools: Powerful & brief /
John Winslade, Gerald Monk.
        p. cm.—(Practical skills for counselors)
    Includes bibliographical references and index.
    ISBN 0-8039-6623-7 (cloth: acid-free paper)
    ISBN 0-8039-6617-2 (pbk.: acid-free paper).
        1. Educational counseling. 2. Storytelling—Therapeutic use. 3.
    Interpersonal relations. I. Monk, Gerald, 1954- II. Title. III. Series.
    LB1027.5.W535   1998
    371.4—ddc21   98-25351

This book is printed on acid-free paper.
    00   01   02   03   04   05   7   6   5   4   3   2

Editorial Assistant:	Kristen L. Gibson
Production Editor:	Sherrise M. Roehr
Editorial Assistant:	Patricia Zeman
Typesetter:	Lynn Miyata
Indexer:	Juniee Oneida

Contents

Preface   vii

About the Authors   x

1. What Is Narrative Counseling All About?   1
   We Live Through Stories   2
   A Narrative Counseling Scenario   3

2. Doing Narrative Counseling: A Step-by-Step Guide   20
   Starting Assumptions   21
   Attitudes to Bring Into the Room   28
   Specific Narrative Methods   32

3. Reworking Reputations   51
   The Discourse of Schooling   52
   School Descriptions   53
   The Power of the Teacher   57
   Deficit Discourse   59
   Resistance   64

4. Conversations With Kids Who Are "In Trouble"   67
   Stealing Trouble   68
   Trouble in the Classroom   71
   Combating Abusive Behavior   77
   Truancy Trouble   89

Enrolling a New Student 92
Counseling and Discipline 93

5. **Working in a Narrative Way With Groups, Classes, and Even Communities: Beyond an Exclusive Focus on the Individual** **95**
   Seeking out a Wider Audience to the New
      Story 98
   Building Communities of Concern 100
   Group Work Programs 103
   Working With a Whole Class 107
   Classroom Lessons Built on "Interviewing
      the Problem" 111
   Starting Conversations With a School 114
   Narrative Climate in the School 117

Reading List **120**

A Narrative Glossary **122**

References **125**

Index **128**

Preface

If you do counseling in schools, this book is for you. If you are a teacher interested in ideas for developing more generative conversations with young people in schools, we hope you too will find here ideas that will stimulate your work.

This book arises out of our enthusiasm for narrative therapy. The narrative pot has been bubbling in our part of the world (we live and work in Hamilton, New Zealand) in recent years. It has been heated especially by the creative, bold, and compassionate work of David Epston and Michael White. Others have taken up these ideas in North America and run with them enthusiastically. However, narrative therapy has largely grown within the family therapy tradition. Our concern is that school counselors are not necessarily closely linked to this tradition and that they therefore may be missing out on the news of this fresh approach to counseling. We wanted to address this state of affairs and speak directly to counselors working in schools.

The enthusiasm we want to share is for the creative potential that comes from thinking in terms of a narrative metaphor. The simple but profound notion that stories, rather than hard-nosed realities, shape our lives is at the base of this work. There has been much academic excitement about the possibilities opened up by postmodern or narrative ideas, but there is a need to translate this excitement into ideas for effective and useful practice. Narrative therapy is a bold step in this direction. It is eminently practical and well suited to counseling in schools. We want in this book to make the practical value of these ideas obvious and accessible.

One of the advantages of the narrative metaphor is that it opens up fresh ways to talk about the intimate, daily struggles of young people and teachers to create meaningful and satisfying lives in the midst of institutional demands and pervasive social forces. We believe it offers us considerable leverage for powerful and effective conversations that produce meaningful changes for people in school communities. It also helps us to work with (or to work against) the way we are all positioned by cultural, gender, and economic discourses.

Young people take to narrative conversations, often more easily than adults. They warm to the respect they are shown and to the playfulness with which this approach allows them to address serious problems in their lives. Counselors, in our experience, also enjoy working in a narrative way. They find themselves more energized and less drained by the people with whom they work.

It seems appropriate to tell stories as we talk about a narrative approach to counseling. Therefore, we have liberally sprinkled stories of narrative counseling in action through this book to convey its flavor in a school context. Chapter 1 is, in fact, a story of a counselor's work with one student, interspersed with comments that describe what the counselor is doing. We have also sought to provide clear guidelines for the practitioner of narrative counseling and even sample lists of questions to suggest typical lines of inquiry in a narrative interview. Chapter 2 contains a step-by-step outline of how to do narrative counseling. In Chapter 3, we pick up on some specific aspects of school discourse and outline some ways of achieving redescriptions of the typical labels that get ascribed to young people in school. In Chapter 4, we concentrate on the particular counseling needs of young people who are "in trouble" at school. Chapter 5 ends the book with an expansion beyond the individual. Here, we consider ways of working with significant others, groups, "communities of concern," whole classes, and even with a whole school community.

This book is grounded in our own work with young people in schools, but it is also grounded in the stories we have shared with our students at the University of Waikato, where we work as counselor educators. Many of them have been highly creative in the work they have done as school counselors, and their stories have both instructed us and enlivened this book. We would like to acknowledge Aileen Cheshire, Dorothea Lewis, Donald McMenamin, Pamela Gray-Yeates, Elizabeth Jordan, Coral Stuart, Nigel Pizzini, and Ian Frayling for some of the specific examples we have used, as well as the young people with whom they have worked, whose stories are represented in these pages. Jeffrey Kottler was highly influential in the conception of this project, and we acknowledge his encouragement and support. Donald McMenamin, Aileen Cheshire, Rolla Lewis, Jeffrey Kottler, and Heather-Ann Monk have also helped us by reading and commenting on earlier drafts of the book. We also acknowledge our colleagues at the University of Waikato, Wendy Drewery, Kathie Crocket, and Wally McKenzie, with whom we share a larger project of developing narrative and social constructionist thinking in counseling. This book is a small part of that project.

JOHN WINSLADE
GERALD MONK
Hamilton, New Zealand

◆ ❖ ◆

This book is dedicated to:
Christine, Benjamin, Zane, Joanna,
Ana, Felicity, and Rian.

◆ ❖ ◆

About the Authors

John Winslade is Senior Lecturer in counselor education at the University of Waikato. His background is in teaching, school counseling, and marriage and family counseling. He also has a strong interest in mediation. He is one of the editors and principal authors of *Narrative Therapy in Practice: The Archaeology of Hope* (1997). He has published articles and taught workshops on narrative therapy and mediation in New Zealand, the United Kingdom, and the United States.

Gerald Monk is Director of the Counselor Education Program at the University of Waikato. His background is in teaching and educational psychology. He has had a private practice as a therapist, where he has worked with narrative ideas over many years. He began introducing narrative therapy as the primary approach taught in the Master of Counselling degree at the University of Waikato in 1993. He is an editor and one of the principal authors of *Narrative Therapy in Practice: The Archaeology of Hope* (1997). He has published articles and taught workshops on narrative therapy and mediation in New Zealand and the United States.

What Is Narrative Counseling All About?

R on, a new school counselor at a high school in Hamilton, put this sign on his door.

PROBLEM BUSTERS

Services offered include:

- Lingering suspensions exterminated
- Bad reputations reversed
- Youth to adult conversions undertaken
- Boredom alleviated
- Trouble silenced

■ Treaties with parents/teachers drawn up
■ Miscellaneous problems gassed, poisoned, shot,
   and/or gotten rid of

Our Motto:

The problem is the problem
The person is not the problem

Not surprisingly, conversations that students had with Ron in his office often took on a weird, yet creatively intriguing, quality. There were some curious comments about the sign. One student asked what it meant. Ron was happy to explain his preference for seeing people as struggling under the weight of problems rather than being problems in themselves. He talked about how he saw blaming people for their problems often immobilized them with guilt and shame and got in the way of change. He described counseling as trying to find a fresh way to talk about problems so that they started to dissolve. The sign on the door was indicative of his ideas about this fresh way of speaking. It carefully focused on the problem as the enemy and the person as separate from it.

Although he was not saying so in so many words, Ron had a passion for using narrative approaches to counseling. They fitted so closely with his own beliefs. What stood out for him was the deep respect for people embodied in the way of speaking that narrative counseling approaches offered.

We Live Through Stories

◆ *We live our lives according to the stories we tell ourselves and the stories that others tell about us.*

Narrative counseling is a deceptively simple therapy. It is based on the idea that we all generate stories to make sense of ourselves and of the circumstances of our lives. However, we are not the sole authors of our stories. Many of the *dominant stories* that govern our lives were generated in our early experiences of childhood at home, at school, at church, and in the neighborhood. These local institutions are in turn given shape by the stories that are current in the wider social contexts in which we live. Some of these dominant stories regularly influence what we think about ourselves. Often, these stories create problems for us. Another way to say all this is that a narrative perspective locates problems in the cultural landscape, which implies that a counselor who is seeking to help needs to consider his or her own and the client's cultural positioning.

If we are located in a story line as "dumb" at school, as "mischievous," or as a "bad egg," there is a tendency to live our lives according to the contours of a problem story laid out before us by such a description. These character descriptions often stick like glue. How does one extricate oneself from the personal description "conduct disordered," or "learning disabled," or "emotionally disturbed"? What effect do such descriptions have on a person? How would one go about giving up identities like these, which follow a person around on report cards and in the minds of teachers?

In part, this book is about addressing the issue of the child who has a problem identity, or possesses the kind of reputation that yields few options about how to live with any sense of personal value and pride in a school community.

A Narrative Counseling Scenario

As a way of introducing narrative counseling, we want to present a counseling scenario that occurred at Ron's school when we were writing this book. This will give you a feel for what a narrative counselor attempts to do with clients. It conveys the spirit of what narrative work is about, as well as illustrating some of the techniques and skills used. In later chapters, we will go back and explain more fully how to develop a narrative counseling conversation. We will also show how to apply this approach in a variety of different circumstances. But first let us tell you a story.

Alan was a ninth-grade student at a high school in Hamilton. He had a reputation as a "troublemaker," which followed him around the school like a shadow. By the eighth grade, he had been nearly suspended twice from school. At the beginning of his ninth-grade year, his reputation preceded him and was quickly gathering some momentum of its own. Alan was, according to three of his teachers, refusing to work in history, math, and social studies. He shouted, argued, and left the classroom without permission. By the third week of the new school year, Alan had nearly worn out his welcome. "Troublemaker" appeared to be worn on his sleeve.

At home, Alan would tease his sisters and argue a little with his Mom, but he was also adored by her. Judy, his mother, had attended many parent-teacher meetings and had taken particular pleasure in pointing out how Alan was a very good boy at home, a little mischievous maybe, but not really badly behaved. She knew that Alan had really struggled at school in some of the early grades. He just didn't seem to fit. His two younger sisters had seemed to adjust to school easily, but school had always seemed somewhat foreign to Alan.

For 2 straight years at school, Judy said, Alan had had trouble trying to relate to a couple of his teachers. He just couldn't adjust to what the teacher was wanting. He couldn't work out what he needed to do to be called successful. It seemed like he was an alien in the culture of the school.

Alan was sitting with his head down in Ron's office, having been referred to counseling as a last resort, and wearing the same defeated expression he had been showing since the new school year had begun. A small scowl was etched into the right corner of his mouth. It threatened to occupy his whole jaw.

Ron was never one to waste words. "I don't work with anybody who doesn't want to work with me."

The match was a perfect one for Alan, although Ron didn't know it yet. Before Alan had a chance to think about answering, Ron continued in the same matter-of-fact tone, "Do suspensions work for you?"

Alan shrugged, "I dunno." The reply had a beaten-down, defeated, flat quality.

Ron had a strong respect for young people's right to speak about what was happening to them. He wanted to hear Alan's conclusions about what he was making of his life. Usually, it is the other way around. Young people are more typically the objects of study by adults and are often excluded from examining their own purposes, reviewing the consequences of their actions, or discussing the effects these actions have on others. Adults often do this work for them and hand them ready-made conclusions.

Because young people are given so few opportunities to reflect upon and evaluate themselves and their circumstances, many of them "don't know" when asked about important things. People like Alan "did know a lot," but to get access to their knowing is a challenge for even a skillful counselor. However, Alan hadn't completely given up on trying to adjust to the culture of the school and the institutional demands it put upon him. The school's prescriptions of etiquette didn't have much appeal for him, but he still objected to being thought of as a troublemaker.

Ron was already warming to this perceptive young man. Alan's hair was bleached by the sun. His face was freckled and somewhat weather-beaten and he looked a little older than his years. Ron generally took a liking to most of the students who came to his office. He wanted to know about their hopes, fears, dreams, and some of the pain they had known. He believed that everybody had gifts and abilities, some of which were still waiting to be discovered. To discover Alan's, he would have to win his trust. Without it, it wouldn't matter what counseling approach he used. Unless he could establish this basis of trust, Ron too would be defeated by the troublemaker reputation that Alan had around the school.

◆ *As with any therapy, the establishment of a strong relationship with the client is crucial. All you learned about attending and listening skills in graduate school are necessary for narrative approaches to counseling.*

Narrative counselors are primed to avoid being captured by *totalizing descriptions* of a person's identity, particularly if these descriptions define the person in terms of a problem. Ron refused the option of seeing Alan as Troublemaker. He wanted to hear Alan's account of the problem story. He also wanted to explore the effects of this problem story on Alan and on his outlook on life. At the same time, from the outset he was keenly alert for any fragment or tidbit of information that was not "troublesome" material. Other brief therapists call this "looking for exceptions." Ron was like a detective on the lookout for clues. However, he was not collecting evidence of Alan's crimes in order to prove his troublemaker reputation. Instead, he was seeking out hints of competence, ability, and knowledge that would form a counterstory to the troublemaker story.

◆ *The narrative counselor stays highly sensitive to any information about the client's areas of competence and ability (particularly in relation to the problem concern) that can be stored away and retrieved later in the counseling process. This will be the raw material for the construction of a preferred storyline for the client.*

The previous day, Judy had been called into the school yet again and told to take Alan home for the day. He had sworn at a teacher and was described as very noncooperative. Today, he was very subdued. He was as close to being finished with school as the school was close to suspending him indefinitely.

Ron asked Alan for permission to ask about five questions. He added, "If I get carried away with asking you questions, you must tell me."

They identified a signal that Alan could use if Ron did get carried away with asking too many questions. Ron's persistent yet respectful curiosity about Alan's experience of school got Alan talking. His "I don't know" gave way to a more animated expression.

◆ *The stance of the narrative counselor is one of respectful curiosity. The counselor works at not assuming too much about the client's world of meaning. Respectful curiosity is used to explore both the effects of the problem on the client and how the client is taking action to reduce the impact of the problem.*

Although Alan's demeanor remained serious, he was looking very thoughtful as he answered Ron's questions.

"When did trouble at school first come along?"

"Trouble" had been around Alan since the third grade.

"I just hate it when teachers think they know everything and try and force their ideas on you!"

Ron inquired about Trouble's pattern of entry. It seemed that something would happen that would offend Alan's sense of justice, and agitation would set in. Once agitation reached a certain level, Trouble would make an appearance. Alan talked about when he had gotten together with a couple of friends and was caught shoplifting. He didn't see himself as a "thief," but he hadn't been able to resist the dare from his friends to steal some fishhooks for jagging in the nearby stream. This was when he first came to the attention of the police, who contacted the school. Since then, Alan had been fitting in at school just enough to establish a place on the edge of the mainstream.

The rapport between Alan and Ron had developed quickly. Alan was intrigued by Ron's unusual questions. Ron spoke as if Alan's problems had a life or personality of their own that was separate from Alan, but in relation to him.

◆ *Narrative counselors engage in* **externalizing conversation,** *separating the problem from the person and giving it a name. The effect of this subtle language shift is that clients begin to experience the problem as being sourced from outside themselves. Externalizing conversations open up space for a perspective where blame and shame become less significant.*

Ron externalized Trouble as the problem and explored with Alan the effects Trouble had on him.

"How did being caught shoplifting affect you?" Ron asked.

"I dunno really," Alan said. "It was stink being caught."

"How did being caught affect your relationship with your mother and sisters?" Ron inquired.

"I usually get on really well with Mom," Alan replied, "but when I got caught she was really wild, and I was grounded after school for a month."

As Alan continued to respond to questions about the effects of Trouble on his life, he gained a much fuller awareness of both the upsides and downsides of Trouble. Ron was carefully mapping the story of Trouble. This enabled Alan to flesh out in some fullness the problem-saturated Trouble story. As he listened to himself speak, he was coming to realize the extent to which Trouble was influencing his story.

By now, Ron had used up his five questions and negotiated permission to ask a few more.

◆ *Having named the problem, the counselor asks "mapping-the-influence" questions to explore the relative strength of the problem and the person. The first aspect of these questions maps the influence of the externalized problem on the person. In the process, the client gains a much fuller experience of what the problem has cost him or her and others around him. This is followed by asking about the influence of the person on the problem.*

Ron asked, "Do you think Trouble is getting more strong or less strong?"

"It seems like it is bigger these days," Alan replied, beginning to slump back in his chair.

"Would you say that Trouble is trying to take over your life completely, or are there still places where it hasn't taken charge yet?" asked Ron nonchalantly. He did not want to appear as though he was taking on Alan's own battles. Nor did he want to push him to take a stand against the problem story, although Ron's questions were clearly helping him consider moving in that direction.

It did seem to Alan that his new year at school was just one total disaster. However, specific questioning made it apparent that there were areas in Alan's school life that were not subject to Trouble's dictates. His physical education teacher was a "cool dude" in his eyes. Alan was one of the top surfers on the surfing team, and surfing was one domain where Alan experienced having confidence and control. He just loved surfing. It was his passion, and as far as Alan could tell, that was what he lived for!

Life wasn't quite so excruciating in his English class, either. His English teacher was young and enthusiastic and could make even small aspects of learning seem relevant. In fact, in English and physical education, Trouble was barely present. Instead, something else was, something like a good relationship with a teacher.

Ron was now switching the attention of the interview. His narrative focus was on the domains in Alan's life where Trouble did not dominate. There were many areas of life where Trouble barely had a look-in or was absent altogether. Ron questioned Alan closely on these areas for some time.

"Alan, how come Trouble doesn't get you in these classes?" asked Ron, looking for a way to prize open a new story that was not dominated by problems.

"Well, it does sometimes. Yesterday, I didn't do one of the essays I was supposed to do. I was reading a surfing magazine. Miss Davies went ballistic."

"Okay," said Ron, recognizing that developing a more favorable story often requires three steps forward and two steps backward. "Have you experienced any times when Trouble was about to take over and you called a halt to it?" Ron asked.

"Well . . . yeah . . . I suppose so," said Alan, slowly and thoughtfully.

◆ *The counselor selects for attention any experience, however minute and insignificant to the client, that stands apart from the problem story. These fragments of experience are the raw material from which the new story can be fashioned. By asking questions about these* **"unique outcomes"** *(White, 1989a), the counselor inquires into the client's influence on the life of the problem.*

"When Miss Davies went off her head, I was real calm and didn't react at all."

"Was that surprising to you?" Ron asked.

"Well, yeah, a couple of my friends were expecting me to blow up and I didn't. I think I was a bit surprised myself."

"How did you manage not to blow up? That would have been a good invitation to do so."

"I dunno," said Alan.

Ron had heard this answer before, but he believed it might be an important thing for Alan to come to know. He wanted to draw out from Alan some explanation about how he could on occasions not rise to the bait. Such knowledge might be very useful to Alan if he could make it available in the situations where Trouble was more influential. So Ron was persistent. He believed that Alan had some competencies that he had not yet storied, nor had they even been given a rich enough description that they were recognizable to Alan as competencies at all.

"Well, what does that tell us about your ability to control this problem? You know, some teachers think you have a short fuse and just 'go off' without thinking or caring about the consequences, but that didn't happen yesterday. What do you think you did?"

"I dunno," Alan repeated, taking more time. Clearly, he was engaged in wondering about himself rather than giving an answer that fobbed Ron off. He was thinking about how sometimes he could stop things from getting worse.

◆ *Persistent questioning and close listening are needed to bring into focus easily discounted or overlooked details of competence or achievement. The counselor needs to maintain a faith that these competencies can be identified, even at times when the client is having difficulty seeing them.*

Because they had now established this moment as one in which Alan had clearly made a decision not to react as Trouble would have required, Ron focused on unpacking this moment. He was interested in the tiny fractals of experience and thought that went into staying calm and not reacting.

"Was it something you said to yourself that got you to settle when Miss Davies went ballistic?"

"Maybe," said Alan thoughtfully. "I think I just block out the words. It was like when I cut my leg surfing a couple of months ago, and when I went to the doctor's, the nurse injected some stuff into my foot and I just breathed and blocked out the pain. I think I probably did something like that with Miss Davies."

Ron's inquiry into the moment of decision had now yielded a connection in Alan's thinking with another moment in time. This connection held out the promise of a credible story of competence, because the ability to do this blocking-out could no longer so easily be explained away as just a chance event. It had now happened at least twice. Alan's answer had also thrown up the metaphor of "breathing and blocking out pain," which could be used again. Ron picked up on this metaphor and wanted to explore its usefulness in changing some of the negative encounters Alan was having with other teachers.

◆ *Having established some recent unique experiences that are not problem bound, the counselor invites the client to develop an explanation of the significance of these experiences. In this way,* **the plot of the alternative story is thickened** *and thematic links between different events are drawn. This works best when there are a few unique experiences that have been identified.*

Ron asked about the connection between blocking out attempts by others to wind him up and blocking out the pain when he received the injection. Alan thought there was a connection. Ron wondered whether getting older and more mature had something to do with developing this ability to block angry reactions sometimes and not let fly. Alan thought that maturity definitely had something to do with it.

Ron then asked a challenging question: "Does it interest you more to stay on the side that is trying to defeat Trouble, or would you prefer to let Trouble carry you along with it sometimes?"

Alan returned to his favorite line, "I dunno."

Ron stayed with this conversation. He felt he was getting close to an important turning point.

"I was just wondering whether your growing maturity and being your own person was the beginning of taking a stand against Trouble. Was it an effort to be in the driving seat of your own life, or are you content to be a passenger? Are you happy to let Trouble steer you in the direction it chooses, or are you perhaps getting yourself ready to take charge of the steering wheel?"

◆ *A crucial phase in the narrative interview is where the client is given an opportunity to judge for himself or herself whether to continue to live by the problem-saturated story or to locate himself or herself in an alternative story.*

Alan was clear that he did want to be in charge of his life and had no interest in Trouble dictating its terms to him. Ron invited Alan to help him draw a rough graph of the influence of Trouble and the influence of Maturity in his life over time. They discussed what happened to Trouble when Alan made moves to increase the influence of Maturity. Alan now had a much clearer picture of what the problem had cost him. He also had begun to get a glimmer of a life that was not controlled by Trouble.

Alan agreed to another counseling session the next day to investigate where this new story might take him. Something in Alan had changed. He became more thoughtful about what some of the teachers were doing and how he had been reacting to them. He did not want to be suspended from school. It wouldn't take much at this stage. So many people had made their minds up about him, and they were just waiting for him to put a foot wrong.

However, he felt unsure about how to turn the tide. His life wasn't going entirely in the direction he wanted. Ron had helped him to see that. Sure, he loved surfing and fantasized a lot about living at the beach and surfing all day. Maybe he would become a professional surfer. He didn't need to work. He didn't need to get an education.

On the other hand, he couldn't give his education away just like that, could he? His Mom had worked so hard, and he knew she wanted him to make something of his life. Bombing out of school would not please her. He had wanted to be a builder for a long time. He could do things with his hands. He had loved the chance to be a builder's laborer the previous summer, when he had helped his Uncle Geoff build a house. His uncle had convinced him to become a qualified builder. For this, he would need to make something of his studies and go to college. Alan knew that a lot was stacked against him. He only needed to lose it once and that would be it. The vice principal had told him so.

Ron was experienced enough as a counselor to recognize what Alan was up against. He continued to ask Alan about his overlooked knowledge of how to prevent Trouble from getting the better of him. They identified and explored three or four occasions where Trouble had not run away with him.

◆ *As counseling progresses, the narrative counselor consistently surveys with the client new areas where the alternative story might be growing. It is not always immediately apparent to the client that aspects of the plot of the alternative story are growing. Persistent and respectful curiosity remain important characteristics of the narrative interviewing style.*

Alan was good at managing angry feelings at home. He was the only male in the household and felt the pressure of responsibility to act maturely in this setting. Ron storied with Alan how he had developed his ability to be responsible; to think of others, such as his mom and sisters; and to care for their needs. He could remember his mother saying to him when he was six that he had to be the man around the house, after his father had left home. The memory was as vivid as if it had happened yesterday, including the awful pressure he felt to fill his dad's shoes. He looked back on his life and noted how he had cared for his mother when she was sick and helped sort out arguments between his little sisters. He knew he had a special place in the family.

Ron had discovered that in one whole area of Alan's life, he was entirely responsible and thoughtful. He had been used to managing pressures to which most of his peers had never been subjected. Ron asked detailed questions to flesh out the self-description of Alan acting responsibly and caring for others. Despite some hiccups along the way, this story afforded a very different picture of Alan than anything anyone at school knew about. Together, they decided that it was a story of growing maturity.

◆ *Just as the problem story has had a beginning a long way back in a client's life, so does the alternative story. It is important to detail the history of every relevant competence and ability. Hidden talents do not emerge out of nowhere into the counseling room. Careful questioning about early experiences of these capabilities strengthens the base from which to build a new sense of direction.*

Next, Ron wondered whether this maturity Alan had been developing all of these years could feature more at school. He asked Alan if he was getting stronger or getting weaker or something else. Alan thought he was definitely beginning to grow stronger. Already, that morning in math, he had decided he couldn't be bothered with the pettiness and negativity of the teacher's comments about his incomplete math assignment. He felt good about not having been wound up like he might have been the previous day.

Ron asked him what that said about his ability to beat Trouble. Alan liked thinking about it in this way. Ron went on, "If that continued, what predictions would you make about Trouble's future?"

Alan was confident that Trouble would become unemployed. Clearly, he wanted to give Trouble the slip. The obstacle that still remained in his way was the reputation he had acquired. It takes a school a long time to revise its views of troublemakers when they have created much havoc and put burdens on already overstretched teachers. Some teachers have long memories, and positive changes so often get missed in the hurly-burly of school life. There was also the question of his reputation with his peers. Some of his friends had a vested interest in watching him stir the pot with teachers they didn't like.

Ron checked with Alan about his old reputation. "Does it still fit, or have you worn it out and do you need a new one?"

Alan thought he was ready for a new reputation.

"So, what kind of a reputation are you seeking?"

Alan said that he wanted a reputation as "somebody who could achieve." After all, he had achieved in some areas that really counted for him. He was one of the best surfers in the school. Moreover, he wasn't that bad in English and could probably make a go of it, if he knuckled down.

Ron asked his favorite narrative question, "Out of all of the people you know, who might not be surprised to hear about the changes you have been making and the plans you have to build a new reputation for yourself?"

Alan quickly identified his mom as the person who would be least surprised with the new decisions he was ready to put into action at school.

"Who else would not be surprised?"

Alan thought of Robert, one of his surfing friends, a quiet guy who really looked up to Alan. He thought Alan had been "stuffing around" and had never quite accepted some of the crazy stuff that Alan had gotten up to. He knew underneath that Alan actually took life pretty seriously. Alan thought that both his mom and Robert would be on his side in building his reputation as an achiever.

Ron asked, "Among your teachers, who would most likely first notice your efforts to reduce the level of trouble in your life?"

Alan thought that Miss Davies would notice. He thought that she "kind of" liked him. Ron and Alan then discussed what exactly these people may have already noticed. Ron said, "If I asked them to write a reference for you, what sort of things would they write?"

They went on to discuss Alan's plans for building his new reputation, a task that he thought best to do slowly, so that he didn't shock too many of his friends, or the teachers, for that matter.

◆ *Counseling does not stop with the development of a desire for a new identity in the client. From a social constructionist perspective, identities are not the sole property of the person to whom they are attached. It is crucial, therefore, that the story being authored in the counseling room is anchored out into the social world in which the client must live. Therefore, the counselor asks questions about the management of the client's reputation. An* **appreciative audience** *to new developments is deliberately sought out. For most of us, it is not possible to make radical changes in our lives without somebody cheering us on.*

Ron asked Alan what difference this new reputation might make to his life. Alan thought it would mean the difference between being a surf bum and somebody who was also into being successful in business. So, one of the effects of this new reputation was that he could now seriously think about being a qualified builder.

Ron expressed a desire to meet with Alan at the end of the week to keep in touch with Alan's plans for himself. He warned that Trouble would be likely to make a comeback, and they discussed ways of dealing with Trouble if it made a reappearance. Alan looked confident that he could deal with it.

Ron, however, knew from experience that it was useful to expect a relapse from the alternative story. He asked Alan where Trouble was most likely to strike and catch him off guard. What combinations of events did Trouble most enjoy? What were Alan's weakest moments likely to be? This conversation proved invaluable, as it turned out. Alan lost it in math on Thursday. He swore at the teacher and walked out of the classroom. His math teacher, Clarky, had given up on Alan. As far as he was concerned, once someone was a troublemaker, he was always a troublemaker. At the end of the week, Alan was downcast. He had been banned from the math class.

◆ *Changing one's reputation in a school is a massive task. A preferred story has to be worked at. The audience that witnessed the performance of the old story take a while to adjust to the fact that things have changed. It is important to prepare the client ahead of time for the problem's attempts at a comeback.*

The vice principal was prepared to let Ron assist Alan, but time was running out. Alan had 2 weeks to shape up or ship out.

"Well, who won out this week when you tally up the results? How many wins for you, Alan, and how many wins for Trouble?" asked Ron.

Alan hadn't quite thought about it in those terms. "Well, I guess Trouble won," said Alan, feeling defeated.

"Well, let's take a close look at the score," Ron said quietly. "I haven't seen you for four days. How many times do you think Trouble got the better of you?"

"Probably about twice," Alan said quietly.

"How many times did you get the better of Trouble?" Ron said evenly.

"I dunno."

"Well, let's look at the number of classes that you attended and let's rate them as to the extent to which you were stronger over Trouble and where it went for your weak points."

As they tallied up the experiences of the week, Alan was considerably ahead. He had been different in many of his classes. There were no problems in Physical Education or English. Even Social

Studies and History were fine. There were no complaints about Alan coming from these classes, and he certainly didn't recall losing it with any of his teachers except Clarky! Yet the troublemaker reputation was intact with the vice principal. Despite his victories over Trouble, Alan was feeling somewhat disheartened.

Ron didn't hook into the despair. He stated quietly, "So, do you think it is going to be Trouble's victory? Do I sense you letting Trouble have the prize? Has it talked you into defeat when you virtually won the first round?"

Alan did not want to give up. There was too much fight in him for that. He had learned that at home. Some therapists might have labeled Alan's home life as dysfunctional or described Alan as code-pendent in his relationship with his mother. Ron was more interested in how Alan's life experience might have been an asset rather than a liability.

For the remainder of the session, they strategized about how Alan was going to inoculate himself against Trouble.

By Wednesday the following week, Alan popped in excitedly, saying that he hadn't lost his cool when Clarky had barked at him in the lunch break. Ron wondered whether Alan was open to letting a few more people into his plans to achieve at school. For example, would he mind if Ron circulated a letter informing some key teachers about Alan's efforts at developing a new reputation? Alan was intrigued but wanted to see the letter first. With Alan's help, Ron crafted a document that described precisely what Alan wanted known about himself.

Ron handed Alan the letter and suggested that he show it to his teachers and note their comments so that he and Ron could talk about their responses next Friday. The letter said:

To whom it may concern:

   I would like to bring you up to date with some developments that have been taking place in Alan Brown's life. As you know, Trouble had been having its way with Alan over an extended period of time and had given him a bad reputation as "Trouble's maker." It had occupied significant areas of Alan's life. It caused him to:

- Swear at teachers
- Walk out of class
- Argue when corrected

I am delighted to report that Alan has been progressively [though humbly and quietly at first] dealing with Trouble in important areas of his life.

He has been seeking to take charge of his life at school and curb Trouble's effects. He favors being in the driver's seat of his own life and letting Trouble take a backseat.

Alan has allowed me to bring these developments to your attention. Our hope is that you will support Alan's efforts to move toward a Trouble-free life at school. We would greatly appreciate you noticing Alan's victories over Trouble.

Best wishes from,
Ron James and Alan Brown (fighters for a Trouble-free life).

The following Friday when they met again, Alan expressed how surprised he had been at some of the positive responses he had had from teachers. Only one of them had seemed to regard the letter as a challenge to catch Alan out and prove that he was still a trouble-maker.

Ron handed Alan a certificate, presented on gold card (see Box 1.1). Alan was barely restraining himself from grinning with satisfaction.

◆ *The weight of the written word is well known to most of us. Statements written on our school record keep a reputation alive. Narrative letter writing recognizes the importance of the written word and uses it in the most positive way. A letter that* **documents the changes** *clients have been making strengthens the significance of the changes in their own and others' eyes.*

Last we heard, Alan was staying with his new reputation of "mature achiever," and it seemed like it was beginning to stick for the people who count, including the vice principal. Not only was Alan still at school, but he was also making steady progress. As for Trouble, Alan admits to the occasional nostalgic trip down Trouble's

---

BOX 1.1

This certificate is to affirm and celebrate that

▨ Alan Brown has made it his business to achieve greater maturity in his life.

This certificate makes public the fact that

▨ Trouble has become less strong in Alan's life as Alan has become more and more mature.

This certificate predicts that

▨ (Apart from an occasional nostalgia show for old time's sake) Trouble will make fewer and fewer appearances until it is simply a thing to be remembered.

This certificate attests that

▨ It is to the credit of Alan Brown that this important change has occurred.

With sincere congratulations!
Ron James
Official observer of important events,
Hamilton High School

---

lane, but nothing that gets him into the vice principal's office. His English has improved a lot. When he is given the chance, he has some great surfing stories to tell.

We have told you a narrative counseling story in order to convey the flavor of this approach. In this chapter we have kept explanatory comments to a minimum in order to allow the story to speak for itself. In the next chapter we will work the other way around. Our aim will be to describe in an accessible way the basic ideas and skills of narrative counseling along with some much briefer examples as illustrations.

Doing Narrative Counseling
A STEP-BY-STEP GUIDE

In the story told in Chapter 1, you may have been intrigued (even puzzled) by some specific question or response the counselor used. It is our task in this chapter to make more sense of these responses so that (if you find them appealing) you can learn to use them. We want to introduce you to a narrative approach to counseling in a step-by-step fashion. Any breaking down of a complex process into steps runs the risks of oversimplifying or falsely implying an inevitable linear progression. However, it also facilitates the learning process, as long as we keep in mind that there is really no foolproof recipe for the complexities of counseling conversation. This chapter aims to provide you with a learning guide, rather than a recipe. We hope you can keep an ear open for the spirit of narrative counseling as you read, rather than seek a technology to copy.

Narrative counseling is founded in postmodern thinking, rather than in liberal social analysis or humanistic psychology. It is not alone in this regard. The postmodern turn in social science thinking has influenced many writers in recent years to revise traditional thinking in the counseling field. To make sense of this work, you do need to entertain some ideas that depart from convention, rather than simply learn to apply some techniques. Therefore, we propose to outline for you

- Some starting assumptions
- Some ethical attitudes
- Some specific methods

However, we don't want to separate these out into chapters on theory, ethics, and skills, because we believe they all interlock. A narrative approach to counseling is more than a new skill modality. It can be dangerous if approached as a set of fancy tricks or techniques. It is partly a consistent ethical stance, which in turn embodies a philosophical framework. Therefore, a counselor's narrative facility benefits as much from grasping some ideas as from learning some techniques. To do this work you need to think in a certain way. The methods flow from this way of thinking.

Starting Assumptions

A narrative approach involves entering a counseling situation with a particular bunch of ideas in mind. Let us acknowledge the origins of these ideas. They have been pieced together into what is now called narrative therapy principally by Michael White and David Epston. However, they draw significantly from themes developed by some scholars from different fields—ethnographers such as Edward Bruner; psychologist Jerome Bruner; French historian of systems of thought Michel Foucault; and biologist and systems theorist Gregory Bateson. From these and other sources, a set of ideas coalesced that gives rise to a coherent practice.

1. Human beings live their lives according to stories.

At first sight, this statement seems unremarkable. We all know that people in all cultures respond to stories, and many counseling approaches encourage clients to tell their story. Edward Bruner (1986), the ethnographer who studied diverse indigenous and Western cultures, argued that people do not just tell stories about real experiences. He put it around the other way and said that the stories we tell about ourselves, and that others tell about us, actually shape reality. In an important way, stories become the reference points for living. Another way of saying this is that stories do not just describe what we see. They construct what we see. Thus, in schools, stories about what constitutes a successful member of the school community (and, just as powerfully, stories of failure) do not just describe children's lives. They actively shape children's experiences of themselves and of school.

2. The stories we live by are not produced in a vacuum.

This is an argument against a primarily individualistic psychology. It suggests that the stories that most powerfully constitute or shape our experience are seldom invented by a single person. They are products of conversations, often many conversations by many people, in a social context. Our subjective experience may often feel like it is ours to own. However, much of it is produced out of the stories that float around in the cultural soup in which we swim. Therefore, in order to understand our clients, it is as important to listen for the stories that are not of their own making but that function to make them up as it is to listen to their experience of those stories.

3. Embedded within stories lie discourses.

Discourse is a word for what gets exchanged in conversation. However, it has also developed another, more specialized usage in recent years. We have begun to talk, not just about discourse in general but about a specific "discourse" (e.g., a discourse of femininity, or of school discipline) or a number of "discourses" (Foucault, 1979). This usage refers to the clusters of taken-for-granted assumptions that lie just beneath the surface of many conversations in a particular social context. These assumptions might be given voice in a set of statements about what is normal or conventional.

For example, the discourse of families with adolescents features assumptions like, "It is normal for teenagers to go through a period of rebellion and to seek to separate themselves from their parents." The influence of an assumption like this can be traced through professional family therapy literature, political rhetoric about provision of youth services, parent-teacher interviews at school, and peer conversations among adolescents. Such a discourse has tangible and material effects in people's lives. It shapes their choices, values, feelings, and actions. It is not a false assumption, because its "reality" is proved by many interactions in many families every day. Because of this, it is hard sometimes to see it as a *cultural assumption* rather than as something hardwired into the psychology of adolescents. Indeed, the only way to do this is from a different cultural perspective. One way to achieve this different perspective is to look back in history to a time when "adolescence," as we know it, didn't exist. People went straight from being children to being adults and didn't move out of their parents' orbit when they did so.

As *Pakeha* (white) New Zealanders, we have also had to learn about the cultural origins of this assumption from the perspective offered to us by Maori New Zealanders. In Maori culture, the whole constellation of family relationships is patterned differently, so that adolescence does not necessarily feature the same stage of rebellion. Separation from *whanau* (extended family) would not be spoken of at all in terms of normal maturation processes. This picture is complicated because of the dominance of the cultural ideas embodied in mainstream psychological knowledge, usually without acknowledgment of their cultural origins. This dominance affects the extent to which young urban Maori families draw from indigenous cultural patterns or from those sanctioned as "normal" by mainstream psychology.

School counselors will frequently talk with students about the development of their lives in ways where the dominant discourse about adolescence will be evident. Therefore, we might say that the lives of teachers and counselors and children are shaped by the discourses that circulate in school communities. They shape what we expect of ourselves and of others around us. They shape our actions and reactions to the events of our lives. They are not the same as "belief systems," which are held by individuals. Discourses are social phenomena that live in the talk that we hear and repeat.

4. *The modern world is characterized by societal norms that are kept in place by surveillance and scrutiny.*

Michel Foucault (1973) called this effect **"the gaze."** This is the requirement to subject ourselves to a comparative and evaluative scrutiny and to learn to see ourselves, not through our own experience, but through the eyes of this scrutiny. For example, whenever we worry about how we appear or come across to others, we can become aware of the gaze at work. As children go through school, they often develop an intense consciousness of how they appear to others. This is a product of such scrutiny. In fact, schools often have highly sophisticated systems for measuring the worth of a person and letting him or her know what kind of a person he or she is: for example, tests, exams, report cards, references, and filing and recording systems. Worries about the effects of such systems are not just individual foibles that can be dismissed by encouragements to "be ourselves" or "think more rationally." The gaze includes the hidden scale of judgment against which we measure ourselves when we entertain such worries. The gaze, and our responses to it, becomes implicated in many of the problems in our lives.

For example, if our body shape does not match the dominant cultural ideas about a beautiful body, we can learn to view ourselves as unattractive. In the West, the triangular-shaped body of an Olympic swimmer for a man, or the tall, skeletal shape of an Italian fashion model for a woman, serve as the norms against which we are daily encouraged to measure ourselves. Through the eyes of such a gaze, we judge ourselves as ugly, lazy, lacking self-control, or undesirable because of the tyranny of such norms. It is not surprising that young women are especially vulnerable to extreme eating problems like anorexia or bulimia. Some young men can also be at risk of steroid abuse as they attempt to mold their bodies to fit dominant cultural expectations about attractiveness. Eating problems can start in young children as soon as they learn to see their bodies through others' eyes. Yet even when eating problems do not develop, many young people, in high schools especially, are affected by the workings of the gaze to engender feelings of inadequacy about their bodies that influence their participation in sport and physical education classes, and their social relationships in the school. Some will weaken their ability to concentrate on learning through excessive dieting.

Of course, the effects of the gaze or cultural assessment go far beyond tormenting the body. Self-scrutiny touches every area of our lives and is thus of central focus for the narrative counselor, who is mindful of the power of discourse to induce us to believe things about ourselves. The gaze also operates in schools through the systems of evaluation and assessment, which serve to classify and categorize young people according to their intellectual performance or their social acceptability. Out of these evaluations, young people construct their beliefs about who they are and what they are capable of. In some counseling theories, this discovery of self emerges from within. From a narrative perspective, what lies within is constructed from without.

5. *There are always contradictory or alternative discourses with which some align themselves.*

Despite the fact that dominant discourses wield an enormous influence on our self-evaluations, there exist contradictory or alternative discourses with which we sometimes align ourselves. Many people do not live by or adhere to dominant cultural specifications and develop pride in choosing to live by alternative cultural patterns. Take, for example, the extent to which people with a gay or lesbian sexual orientation publicly and proudly declare their sexuality in communities where strong views about heterosexuality prevail. Yet this stance initially comes at great cost. There are often painful consequences for those who challenge the authority of dominant cultural stories. Children whose parents are living a gay or lesbian lifestyle can easily have such painful consequences visited upon them. In school, they are reminded of their difference every time they are given a form or a letter to take home that presumes a "normal," two-parent, heterosexual, family environment.

6. Dominant cultural stories impose severe limits on people
seeking to create change within their lives.

People are often unaware of how discourses restrict their knowledge and volition about how to think and act. Hence, alternative or preferable ways of living can remain hidden. For example, a boy might be strongly influenced by traditional male discourses to act tough, be unemotional, assert his will over others, and be competitive at any cost. Even when these ideas about how to be male put him in conflict with his teachers or with other students, he may never question whether he could be any different.

7. Deconstructing dominant discourses raises new
possibilities for living.

Counseling can provide an opportunity to take apart, or unpack, discourses and reveal their impact on a person's life. This is the process known in narrative counseling as **"deconstruction"** (White, 1992). The counselor might ask:

- Does this situation invite you to react in particular ways?
- What ideas do you have about _____ that explain why you acted that way?
- How did you learn them?
- From where did you get the ideas that invited you to take that action?
- Has this approach always worked best for you?
- Who in your life supports this way of doing things?

These kinds of questions invite a client to examine the cultural content of the stories that are prominent in his or her life and to evaluate their effects. Recognition often follows that there is not an inevitability about the way life has been going. The flip side of such recognition is that possibilities for how life might be otherwise become apparent. As the client considers these possibilities, the counselor can ascertain whether the client would prefer to continue with the status quo or whether he or she wants something different for himself or herself.

8. There is always lived experience that does not get encapsulated in stories.

Many problem-bound stories gather momentum because people adjust to the growing discomfort of problems that increases slowly over time. Because people are so close to problems, they often fail to perceive the trends in which their circumstances are embedded. When a problem trend is carefully storied, most people gain a much fuller recognition of their circumstances. They are then in a better position to notice changes in the effects of the problem story upon them. Moreover, noticing such changes, even tiny ones, tends to inspire greater willingness to address their circumstances in ways that they were not able to do before. As a result, narrative counselors seek to work with clients to situate a problem in a historical context. They ask questions about how long the problem has been around and what has happened to it over time. Such historicizing sets the stage for noticing new developments.

Edward Bruner (1986) taught us that there are always lived experiences that are not encapsulated in the stories by which we live. Isolated moments of experience always exist outside of the thrall of problem-saturated stories. It is crucial to a narrative approach for a counselor to hold to this belief. The counselor can then elicit from the client these events that contrast with the problem story. They become the building blocks for an alternative, more favored story. For example, there will be aspects of a young man's macho, male story that are not completely satisfying to him. There will also be experiences he has had that were emotionally rich, warmly affectionate, and noncompetitive. Initially, they may be difficult to find, and both the counselor and the client may need to engage in a search to discover them. When found, however, they enable the counselor to draw distinctions between the plot of the problem story and the counterplot of the emerging new story.

9. The task of the counselor is to help the client construct a more satisfying and appealing story line.

Gregory Bateson (1972, 1980) argued that we learn by comparing one phenomenon with another. We know black because we compare it to white. We know hot because we have had the experience of cold.

He suggested that we learn by noticing what he called "the news of difference." Narrative counseling helps clients draw distinctions between one set of experiences and another, usually between a problem story and its *counterplot*. The comparison helps clients evaluate where they want to position themselves. Drawing sharper distinctions delineates clearer choices for clients, who are then able to experience themselves as having the ability to act in a new way.

Attitudes to Bring Into the Room

Optimism and Respect

Narrative counseling is based on a tempered optimism and a thoroughgoing respect for the client. The optimism is about the existence of the necessary knowledge needed to resolve, or at least manage, a problem already within the repertoire of the client. When students come for assistance, counselors can forget that the students bring knowledge with them into the room. It is a fundamental principle of facilitating learning that it is enormously beneficial to find out what a person already knows. When a young person asks for our help, it is tempting to assume that he or she is lacking in the necessary knowledge or skill to address the problem. However, another explanation is that young people are not used to experiencing themselves as authorities on themselves. Often, they are the objects of focus in school, particularly when they are in trouble. They are rarely given the opportunity to review, interpret, and evaluate what is taking place in their lives. They are seldom asked to examine their motives or consider the consequences of their actions. More commonly, they are told by adults what the events in their lives mean.

It is not uncommon for a teacher to hear a student say, "I don't know," when asked a question about some aspect of his or her life. Young people often feel that they have to produce answers to please the adult inquirer. "I don't know" might be a self-protective response that guards the young person from potential humiliation and ridicule. Sometimes, too, it means "I don't care" or "You don't have the power to make me tell you what I know."

To be effective with narrative counseling, the counselor should view the young person as someone who has knowledge, but may never have had encouragement to access his or her own ability to make sense of the problem. Giving a person this kind of respect calls forth hidden resourcefulness and promotes a respect-full relationship.

Curiosity and Persistence

To begin to enter the young person's world requires of the counselor passionate curiosity. Counselors learn most about their clients when they enter into conversation in a spirit of naïveté, or from a position of "deliberate ignorance" (Hoffman, 1992). They communicate that they do not know the world of the young person but are intently curious to find out. Even when the young person responds with "I don't know," counselors need to be respectfully persistent and creative in generating questions that will ultimately access the young person's knowledge.

Asking questions is typical of a narrative counselor, but they are not the kind of questions that seek to confirm what the counselor already knows. They are questions asked from a position of genuinely wanting to learn about the meanings of the child's world. This stance prevents the questioning from seeming like an interrogation.

Respect for the Client's Knowledge

Counselors using a narrative approach do not claim there is one true account of life. Therefore, we cannot know and be sure what is in the best interests of our clients. Certainly, we will have some ideas about what we think might help those with whom we work. However, we do not assume that we can give an authoritative account of what must be done. Therapy is an activity that produces meaning from the interactions between actors, each of whom represents her or his own cultural world. These may or may not have a high degree of overlap. Out of respect for the generative potential of conversation, we should not enter it prejudging what will happen.

Working in this way demands of the counselor constant vigilance about imposing his or her own cultural locatedness upon the client. Ethically, the narrative counselor cannot hide behind a truth-based theory of how the world works and a knowing of how human beings function.

Perhaps the major difference between narrative therapy and other counseling traditions is the emphasis on a stance of "tentativeness," rather than knowing. This serves to temper the counselor's judgments from being dogmatically forced onto his or her clients. It guards against the tendency of Western counseling theories to colonize clients' interpretations of life and produce adherents. Rather, the narrative counselor seeks to convey to the client a deep respect for the person's own knowledge, which is likely to be subjugated knowledge, and therefore undervalued. This valuing seeks to subsume generalized professional knowledge beneath particularized, commonsense, or local knowledge, rather than the other way around.

Negotiating Coauthorship

The relationship between the counselor and the client aims to establish a special kind of partnership in narrative counseling. Some aspects of this are not unique to a narrative approach, but some aspects have a distinct flavor in the hands of a narrative counselor. As we have said, it is a relationship founded not on the demonstration of expertise on the counselor's behalf. Nor is it focused only on the discovery of preexisting or dormant knowledge in the mind or heart of the client. A narrative conversation is based on shared contributions to a process of creation. The counselor cannot do it alone; nor can the client. The conversation between them is what produces the effectiveness of the counseling. The counselor must bring to this conversation some special attributes. These include the ability to negotiate the relationship in a way that is inclusive of the client and gives him or her a real say in the counseling process. It should be a real power-sharing dialogue. Box 2.1 shows some things you can do to set up this kind of negotiated relationship.

BOX 2.1

Negotiating a Power-Sharing Relationship

1. Ask the client's permission to ask some questions about the problem rather than assume that because you are the counselor, you automatically have this right.

2. Ask the client's permission to take notes about the session.

3. Offer the client the chance to read the notes you make and any files you keep on the counseling.

4. Don't write anything or say anything to anyone else that you would not be happy for the client to overhear you saying (unless you have the client's permission to do so). Real care needs to be taken with computer databases in this regard.

5. Inquire from time to time whether the counseling conversation you are having is going in the direction the client would like it to go

6. Ask the client if the counseling is proving helpful. If so, ask what is helpful about it, so you can learn from the client how to do your job.

7. Treat the client as knowledgeable and worthy of professional respect, as someone from whom you can always learn.

8. When parents and children are involved in a family interview, treat everybody as having a right to have a voice, rather than speaking to parents over a child's head.

9. Ask for the client's ideas about what might be helpful in dealing with the problem rather than putting on the professional mantle of knowing better.

10. Consult with the client about how progress is being achieved, and ask permission at times to record and document this knowledge so that it may be shared with others (see Chapter 5).

Specific Narrative Methods

Listening to the Problem-Saturated Story
Without Getting Stuck

Many school counselors will have had this kind of experience: A young man walks into your office. He has often been in trouble. He has been told to come and see the counselor but doesn't particularly want to be there. You try to show respect for his feelings and engage him in conversation. He is barely cooperative and doesn't appear interested in sharing his personal life with you. Client-centered listening does not seem to work with him. The conversation becomes quite strained. Against your better instincts, you start to think about how difficult a person he is. You find yourself sympathizing with the teachers who are frustrated with him, and before you know it, you are lecturing him about being more responsible and thinking about his future. His eyes roll upward, and you know that you are wasting your breath. It is easy to blame him at this moment but, in fact, as a counselor, you are stuck.

It is through such experiences that some counselors have come to search for a different way of listening that might give both the counselor and the client in this situation a chance to have a more useful exchange. A narrative counseling style offers such a young man a different place from which to be heard than do counseling approaches that encourage people to take responsibility for their problems. This is achieved through a specific use of language, as we will explore below, but it begins with a specific way of listening.

A narrative counselor begins like many other counselors by engaging with the client to hear the problem story. This involves using the basic relational skills of attending, paraphrasing and clarifying, summarizing, and checking. But there is always a process of selection in the choice of what gets heard and how it is listened to. For example, if a client cries as a result of a hurtful and abusive experience she has endured, there are a variety of ways to listen to this, each of which might be embodied subtly in the attending, paraphrasing, and summarizing. One counselor might respond to the tears as a cathartic expression of repressed feeling and convey encouragement to dwell in the moment of bodily emotional expression. Another may respond to the tears as a function of faulty thinking and convey encouragement to explore the beliefs that lie beneath the feeling. What, then, are the assumptions that a narrative counselor would bring to the process of hearing the problem-saturated story? These assumptions are embodied in the list of suggestions in Box 2.2 for responding as you listen.

An Example. Elaine, 13 years old, had been diagnosed with clinical depression and had been receiving medication for some weeks. Her counselor, Mary-Anne, was having great difficulty engaging with Elaine. So much of the conversation was stilted and awkward. It was difficult for Elaine to concentrate, and at times she seemed vacant and distant. Her voice had a flat quality.

Elaine had been a high-achieving student but over the past 2 months had been missing significant periods of school. Her grades were deteriorating. Her parents had recently separated. Because Elaine had never seen her parents argue or appear unhappy, the announcement of separation had come as an enormous shock. She had believed that she had the most "normal" and "happy" family. Her friends used to envy the togetherness that her family had portrayed. Now, on reflection, her family and all that it stood for appeared to be a sham. Her mother, Deborah, struggled to get Elaine out of bed in the mornings to go to school. Elaine was constantly tired, tearful, and lethargic. Deborah was frightened by the intensity of Elaine's moods and had enlisted the help of the school counselor.

Elaine experienced everything as shrouded in a gray-black cloud. Life right now seemed pointless and empty. She did not want to live and felt like giving up. Mary-Anne was careful to check out the suicide risk, but Elaine did not have any elaborate plans to end her life. Moreover, she contracted to behave safely with herself and to let Mary-Anne know of any changes.

Mary-Anne could not remember working with a student who had presented as so despairing. She was determined not to become paralyzed herself by the spell of depression, although she was aware that it could cover her like a soggy blanket. This required her to attend constantly to her voice, her energy levels, and her sincerity,

BOX 2.2

Listening to the Client's Story

1. As you listen to the story, stay alert for details that relate to the client's competence as well as to oppressive problems.

2. Avoid using totalizing language to describe problems.

3. Hear emotional pain as the effect of what is problematic in this person's world. Explore thoroughly the extent of these effects. Ask the client to name what is causing these effects.

4. Don't rely on cathartic expression to bring about change.

5. Listen for the operation of cultural stories or discourses in the person's problem story.

6. Be alert to how your own positioning in cultural stories predisposes you to hear what others tell you.

7. Begin to separate the person from the problem in your mind as you listen and respond.

8. Listen for the operation of power relations in the construction of the problem.

9. Avoid using internalizing language that implies that the problem is basically an intrapsychic one or the result of a personal deficit in the individual client.

10. Attend to feelings of delight or pride in small achievements of victory in relation to the problem as much as to feelings of anger or grief or despair at the strength of the problem.

11. Listen for ways the problem has tried to hook teachers, parents, and counselors into its dance. Respond to problems by using more than an individual focus.

12. Be aware of the possibility that problems can sometimes overwhelm counselors.

13. Continue to be curious about the problem story. Don't assume that you ever know the full story or even that you know what the meaning of any particular expression is.

without slipping into a forced cheeriness. It proved enormously important to Elaine that Mary-Anne was not consumed by the power of the depression. This enabled Elaine to trust the process that Mary-Anne was coconstructing.

Several things characterize Mary-Anne's listening in this example. She doesn't mistake the depression for the person. In other words, she consistently listens to Elaine's voice and takes seriously her comments about the problem, rather than interpreting all of Elaine's comments within a frame of depression. She disciplines herself to try to understand Elaine's interpretations of what has happened in her family, rather than reading-in what books and journal articles might say about typical factors influencing young people whose parents separate. She assumes that Elaine has the ability to make a difference to depression's grip on her and conveys this in her responses. She also avoids thinking of the problem as a monolith that will dominate her own view of Elaine. She maintains respect for the power of the problem to have effects in Elaine's life, while at the same time listening for evidence of Elaine's power to loosen depression's grip.

Naming and Externalizing the Problem

Narrative counseling is known for the externalizing of problems. This is a rhetorical device developed by Michael White and David Epston (1992) in their work with families. It helps people locate the problem as separate from their identities. The technique was clearly illustrated by the counseling work with Alan in Chapter 1. It is not just a technique in the sense of a gimmick. The narrative belief is that problems actually have their origins in the discourses that surround us and get mapped onto our bodies and into our lives. So externalizing them puts problems back where they belong (see Box 2.3).

Using externalizing conversations opens space to create a lighter and more playful approach to the seriousness of painful problems (Freeman, Epston, & Lobovits, 1997). Locating the problem outside the person reverses the trend in conventional counseling (and much popular psychology) to have the person own the problem, and then take responsibility for it, as a step toward solving it.

BOX 2.3

Examples of Talking in an Externalizing Way
About Some Common School Problems

- Instead of saying, "How did you feel about the teacher shouting at you?" you can say, "So Anger got the teacher to shout at you. What did it get you to do?"
- Instead of saying, "How do you feel about failing that test?" you can ask, "What influence is Failure having on you? Has it attacked your confidence? Does it want you to give up?"
- Ask about powerful social discourses in a way that does not blame any particular person. "In your experience, how much say does Racism have in the school playground?"
- With disclosures of sexual abuse, something like "Secrecy" might be externalized and its effects asked about. For example, you can ask, "How much has Secrecy ruled over you and prevented you from getting help?" This can be experienced as less blaming than, say, "Have you been feeling too ashamed to speak to anyone?"
- In mediating a dispute between two children, or between a pupil and a teacher, a counselor might hear the sequence of events that have happened and then externalize the whole sequence. "So how has that whole cycle of things that went back and forth between you left you feeling toward each other?"

Externalizing conversations can also be said to parody dominant cultural stories, thereby opening up space for new cultural forms to develop. In particular, they parody the deficit thinking (see Chapter 3) that pathologizes people and requires that they embrace a sense of hopelessness, shame, or guilt.

In recent years, the more fluid idea of "developing externalizing conversations" has replaced the idea of simply "externalizing the problem." The idea of externalizing conversations includes a sense of evolving through time. It takes the pressure off counselors to come up with a neat and tidy externalization that will maintain the counseling relationship over time. Instead, it acknowledges that conversations take twists and turns and meet surprises and that people are often caught by multiple problems that all get tangled together.

Suggestions for Developing Externalizing Conversations

1. Don't rush to externalize the first things the client talks about as problematic. Listen carefully to a full enough exploration of the problem to be sure that the externalized description of the problem you develop captures the extent and complexity of the problem.

2. If you feel strange using externalizing language, explain to the client what you are doing. You can say something like, "I sometimes like to look at the problem as something that is outside of you and then ask about the influence it is having on you. I find this helps bring a new perspective on the problem, which can help us find ways to deal with it. Is it OK if we experiment with talking like this for a bit?"

3. Don't worry if you are calling the unexplored problem "it" or "this problem" or "these difficulties." These descriptions give the counselor plenty of time to explore the general issues going on in a client's life without zeroing in too narrowly on one problem domain too quickly.

4. Share the task of naming the problem with the client. You can say something like, "We've been talking for a while about all these things that have been building up at school in the past few weeks. Can we think of a name for this whole problem story that we can use to talk about it? Have you got any ideas for a name for it?"

5. Often, people are not immediately sure what kind of description to give the problem when a problem theme has been sufficiently assembled. Help the person name it by recalling some problem descriptions that other clients have used. On occasions like this, Freeman et al. (1997) suggest asking the young person if the description given

is warm, followed by, "What would be a name that would make it hot for you?"

6. Whatever entry point is used in the naming process, use a description that matches the person's experience of the problem. If a facile description like "argument" is used to encapsulate a complex series of painful experiences of injustice, or serious violation, a lot of damage can be done. A name that is out of step with the client's fuller experience conveys to the client that his or her painful stories have not been heard or acknowledged.

7. If a client brings you a story that features not one but a series of problems, there is a danger that the one you choose to externalize may not be the one that most concerns the client at this time. In order not to focus on a peripheral issue, it is best to ask the person on which issue he or she has most interest in working.

8. Externalizing conversations have their most powerful effect when the externalization reverses the internalizing logic of a piece of taken-for-granted discourse. Emotions like guilt, anger, hurt, embarrassment, or shame are sometimes clues to this kind of logic occurring. Rather than externalizing the emotion itself, ask about what situation is producing this emotional response and then externalize that situation. For example, if a girl is feeling hurt by some rumors that are circulating around the school about her, externalize Rumor and speak about the hurt feelings as being produced by Rumor. If these rumors were to feature judgments of her body as "too fat," it would not be helpful to develop an externalization of "Overeating" because this would locate the problem back in her as an internal lack of willpower or the like. More useful would be to develop an externalizing description of the "Perfect Body Image" that might be infecting the minds of those who spread the rumors and also wreaking havoc on her own self-esteem.

9. With younger children especially, but also with older young people and adults, develop externalizing descriptions into personifications. Michael White's (1989a) well-known story of Sneaky Poo as an externalized personification of encopresis is an example. The

personified problem can have a personality as well as a name. It can be thought of as deceptive and tricky, or hungry and greedy, and as having thoughts and feelings, such as glee when it wins a victory over the child or disappointment and anger when the child scores a victory over it. The personification of problems leads to more dramatic and less abstract conversation about change.

10. When you have developed an externalized description of the problem, embed it into the conversation over a period of time by using it. Start by mapping the effects of the problem on the person. Say something like, "So how has this 'troublemaker reputation' affected you? What has it persuaded other people to think or say about you? How does it convince them of these things? How does it get you to think about yourself? How does it want you to respond?" As the client mentions other thoughts and feelings and actions, these can all be assigned to the designs of the problem.

11. A useful checklist to use in mapping the effects of the externalized problem is to think in terms of the three dimensions of *length, breadth, and depth.*

- **Length** refers to history: "How long has this problem been around?" "When did it start?" "Has it been getting worse or better?" Future effects (if things keep going where they are heading) can also be speculated about. Charts and time lines of the history of the problem story can be drawn up in this process.

- **Breadth** refers to the extent of the problem's empire: "How widely has this problem spread its effects in your life?" "Does it stay at school, or does it come home with you too?" "Does it affect your feelings about yourself all the time or just in your math class?" Areas of a person's life that might be explored to establish the breadth of a problem's regime include feelings and internal experiencing, self-concept, attitudes, relationships, classroom demeanor, family interactions, friendships, study habits, career plans, school achievements, sports, social life, social identifications, and so on.

▓ **Depth** refers to the intensity of the effects of the problem: "How deeply has this problem affected you?" "How heavily does it weigh on you?" "Does the intensity of the problem vary? If so, when is it hardest to handle? When is it easier to handle?" The intensity of a problem's effects can also be graphed by the client and counselor over time, and changes can be linked to events that are happening at the time.

Mary-Anne wanted to understand how the depression invaded Elaine's life and sucked out any feeling of pleasure or happiness. By exploring the effects of depression and the toll it had taken on Elaine, Mary-Anne wanted to create some space between Elaine and the depression so that she no longer felt that there was nothing left of herself that was not completely occupied by depression's spell. She wanted to expose the kinds of strategies and techniques depression used to talk Elaine out of her previous self-description as a happy and outgoing person.

Elaine described being frightened by the overwhelming power of what she named as "IT." Mary-Anne offered to write down Elaine's story on the computer as she told it. Telling the story that way helped capture more clearly depression's attempts to sully Elaine's ambitions. Sitting side by side seemed more comfortable for Elaine. Over the next two sessions, they mapped out when depression had first made an appearance, how it had progressed, and what it had started to make Elaine believe about herself. Depression liked to talk Elaine into blaming herself for her parents' separation. It reminded her of all the times she had brought stress into her parents' lives. It magnified occasions when she had been less than cooperative and responsible. She had always felt so proud of her parents' relationship, because many of her friends were being raised by one parent. Now depression insisted that her life was a lie. It fed on her belief that she had mapped out her life to be like her parents, and now that map had been torn apart.

In all of this work, Mary-Anne consistently externalized, not just the name of the problem, but also the source of all its problematic effects. Some of the questions she asked to map these effects were:

1. What effects has depression had on your:
   - ability to have fun?
   - plans for your future?
   - ability to study?
   - friendships and family relationships?
2. On a scale of 1 to 100, how much of your life has depression taken over (if zero equals not at all and 100 equals completely).
3. What has depression been talking you into that goes against what you have always believed about yourself?
4. What tricks does depression play to get you to feel so miserable?

These questions help to untangle what was a tangled mess of a problem. Problems become tangible, nameable, and beatable as a result. These questions also add to the linguistic separation between the person and the problem. Thoughts and feelings of self-loathing are disrupted by such questions. The steady prizing apart of the person and the problem gives the client a new perspective on the toll the problem has taken. Reduced self-recrimination leaves the young person feeling less weighed down and more able to challenge the problem.

We hope you have noticed the different way of using language that we have illustrated in the above section. If used consistently, it induces a shift in perspective. This kind of conversation does not minimize the strength of the problem in a person's life. It does, however, give the client a greater purchase on the task of managing or disrupting the effects of the problem.

Detecting Clues to Competence

As the externalizing conversation develops, the counselor needs to be alert to the discovery of clues to competence. Like a detective trying to build up a case from what at first seems like little available evidence, a counselor combs carefully through the problem-saturated story for openings to a different story. Sometimes, these pop up in the middle of a conversation and are scarcely noticed by the client because they seem so insignificant. Sometimes, they need to be sought out by deliberately asking for them. These *unique outcomes* (Michael White's, 1989b, term) may be:

- actions
- thoughts
- intentions to act
- moments when the effects of the problem don't seem so strong
- areas of life that remain unaffected by the problem
- special abilities
- knowledge about how to overcome the problem
- problem-free responses from others
- relationships that defy the problem's persuasions

Whenever they do arise, these clues need to be taken up by the counselor and carefully developed, with the client's assistance, into admissible evidence for the case against the problem's continued dominance. Many people learning to work in a narrative way struggle at first to elicit unique outcomes. With some practice, however, counselors can begin to notice openings for alternative stories all over the place. Box 2.4 provides some starting places for this search.

Let us return to Elaine's story as an example. While depression had attempted to suck dry any sense in Elaine of her capabilities and competence, there was another story to be told about Elaine's ability to sustain herself despite the onslaught of "IT." At the next session, the depression seemed unrelenting and Elaine appeared exhausted. Mary-Anne told Elaine that she would not allow the power of depression to whittle away her own hope. Then she asked how Elaine was protecting herself against depression depleting her energy and vitality. They discussed relaxation techniques to help Elaine get more sleep. Mary-Anne then used mapping-the-influence questions (White, 1989b) to map the little ways in which Elaine was having some influence on the problem. These are some of the questions she asked to elicit this story:

- Tell me about the bit of you that depression has not clouded.
- When the depression wants to keep you in bed, how do you eventually get to school?

BOX 2.4

Suggestions for Detecting Clues to Competence

1. Begin by assuming that unique outcomes in the story of the problem do exist, even when they appear hard to find.

2. Discuss with the client his or her relationship with the problem in order to chart any changes.

3. Ask whether the client wants the problem to continue or not. The verbal expression of the desire to defeat the problem may be an important step in developing the resolve to achieve this.

4. Listen for statements that contradict what you would expect the problem to have happening. When you hear these, interrupt and ask more about them.

5. Don't accept too quickly descriptions of events in which the problem seems to have been absent by chance or accident. Given the dominance of the problem, it is all too easy for people to gloss over the significance of their own actions. Inquire closely into what the client might have thought about or done differently on these occasions.

6. If the client is too modest to notice his or her own competence, the counselor or the client can ask someone else (teacher, parent, classmate) to do so.

7. Deliberately ask about occasions when the problem is not around, is not so strong, is in another classroom, on vacation, or less powerful.

8. Distinguish between good intentions the client may have and actions in which these good intentions are subverted by the problem's influence.

■ What do you do to stop the depression from talking to me?

■ What are the hopes you have that stop you from completely giving in to depression?

■ How is that depression has not robbed you of those hopes?

Assembling the Alternative Story

The biggest challenge in constructing an alternative story lies in the contrast between the fragility of the moments of competence and the denseness of the problem story. Problem stories grow over a considerable time and take on lives of their own. They are typically experienced as true accounts of what is happening to the protagonists in the story. In the midst of an ugly situation, the problem story can overshadow all other events. Just as the problem story has grown in strength, so must the alternative story develop a plot that is robust enough to stand up to the problem story's authority. One or two isolated experiences are not going to be sufficient to accomplish the task. Neither is the encouragement and positive talk of the counselor going to make a lasting impression against the full onslaught of the problem.

The skill and expertise of the counselor using a narrative approach lies in carefully assembling, with the client, a story line that is invigorating, colorful, and compelling. The alternative story or counterplot emerges from the use of mapping-the-influence questions, which elicit the preferred experiences, sparkling moments, or unique outcomes. These unique outcomes appear sometimes in a disguised form, and their significance is often discounted by clients. Not only are lived moments the "stuff" of the counterplot, but so are beliefs, attitudes, purposes, hopes, and dreams that support the alternative story. Through deconstructive questioning, the history of these dreams, hopes, beliefs, and purposes can be brought forth. This kind of questioning requires the counselor to be quite active. If the counselor sits back and waits for the client to volunteer the alternative story, the process may slow down and stop. This does not mean that the counselor has to take the role of author out of the client's hands, but it does mean that the counselor should select for highlighting and detailed investigation the aspects of the client's conversation that can serve the purposes of the alternative story. Let us list some ideas to aid this process.

Suggested Lines of Inquiry for Assembling the Alternative Story

1. Pinpoint recent actions that do not fit with the problem story.

2. Ask how the person achieved these actions. Persist with this question even when the client doesn't see himself as particularly agentic or gives someone else the credit. Asking a person to give an account of how he did something assists the person to experience himself as an actor in his own life.

3. Ask about other similar actions in the recent past.

4. Inquire about the thoughts and feelings that preceded and followed these actions. Ask how the person prepared herself to take this action and how she thought and felt afterward.

5. Seek out descriptions of the qualities or values required for such actions.

6. When no completed actions are available, ask about intentions or desires to act.

7. Invite the client to give the counterplot a name.

8. Explore the history of the counterplot in this person's life.

9. Identify other audiences to the counterplot who might have noticed, appreciated, or assisted the person's actions. A useful question is, "Who might not be surprised that you did this?" If someone was surprised, then you can explore how this is a new development. If there is no real surprise, then you can explore what this person might have known all along about your client.

10. Invite speculation about the meaning of these events and of the responses of others.

11. Draw connections between events.

12. Ask whether the young person is pleased with the alternative story and why.

13. Watch for new sparkling moments between counseling sessions.

14. Interrupt talk that drifts back into the problem story.

15. Invite the client to speculate about the direction life would take if the new story continued to develop.

16. Ask about the next steps for which the person might be preparing.

17. Project identities, reputations, and careers into the future and wonder about how they might develop if the new story continues to go forward.

18. In subsequent sessions, map the development of each line of action, thought, or feeling.

Let us return to our illustrative story and show this phase of work in action. Elaine's counselor began to map closely the local knowledge that Elaine had developed in order to feel more like herself rather than depression's self. She became aware of resources she could use to deal with depression when it returned on occasion. There were numerous things she would do to outsmart depression's tactics. One of her favorites was to think about fun things like the taste of mangos, jellyfish fights with her brother, and the pranks she had played on her best friend at her surprise birthday.

Mary-Anne asked whether Elaine realized how powerful her thoughts were to prevent depression from bringing her down.

Elaine commented, "I do now, but I wouldn't have consciously thought about it, if you hadn't asked me."

Elaine had been writing short stories and poetry. The story of depression inspired her to write a poem about her personal struggle. She brought to the next session a beautiful, decorated folder full of her poems and stories. She had written of the serenity of a summer holiday with a favorite cousin. She had written a beautiful account of a sunset. She had recorded the mixture of excitement and fear when caught outdoors in a freak thunderstorm. Mary-Anne used these events as cues for storying Elaine's sensitive and creative talents that depression had not totally suppressed. There was a wealth of sparkling moments that were in stark contrast to the depression story. Mary-Anne asked Elaine where she had developed the acute sensitivities evident in the subtleties of her stories and poems. Elaine could relate these talents back to as early as she could remember. She had always had a fascination for words and their meanings.

"Are these memories on your side," inquired Mary-Anne, "or on depression's side?" Elaine was clear that her creative talents sustained her against the oppression of depression.

Mary-Anne inquired further into how Elaine kept going without being totally consumed by depression, even though some days felt like that.

Elaine recognized that she used to think of her grandfather's indomitable spirit, which had sustained him when Elaine's grandmother had died.

Mary-Anne asked what her grandfather would say about the kind of person she was when she was little. "Would your grandad be surprised to hear the conversation we are having now about how you are beginning to drive depression out of your life?"

These questions led Elaine to redescribe herself as symbolically carrying forward her grandfather's spirit. She felt less alone in her struggle against depression.

Documenting the Evidence

From a narrative perspective, new stories take hold only when there is an audience to appreciate them. Certainly, the client and counselor are the first witnesses to the emergent preferred story. Moreover, new stories can be undermined by others who are expecting a continuance of the old. Thus the creation of an audience to cheer the client on preoccupies much of the work of a narrative counselor.

Often the creation of written documents adds to the impact of the counseling conversation. They serve as a more permanent record of the subject matter of conversation than what the memory can retain. Such documents can be revisited from time to time, and the story that they are part of can be re-inspired. For these reasons, narrative therapists have championed the use of written documents and their circulation in the cause of the new story (White & Epston, 1992).

In schools there are many forms of written communication, often fulfilling institutional requirements and documenting the culture of the school. Problems are more often well-documented than solutions, however. A challenge for counselors operating in a narrative frame is to create ways in which alternative stories can be documented and circulated in the school community.

Here are some ways this can be achieved:

1. Invite significant others to be present at counseling sessions. These can be family members, teachers, or classmates. Ensure that these others are involved in the recognition and appreciation of the new story as it emerges.

2. Compose letters to clients, recording on paper their achievements in overcoming the problem's regime.

3. Work with children to write a letter to teachers or parents.

4. Issue certificates of recognition, or graduation, to celebrate the defeating of specific problems.

5. Draw up report forms that ask teachers to notice the performance of the new story in class.

6. Work with a family to write a story of "taking responsibility" to present to a school board at a suspension hearing.

7. Write an end-of-term report on progress in problem busting.

8. Publish an archive of children's achievements in the face of significant problems in the school magazine or newsletter.

Here is an example of a letter written by Mary-Anne to Elaine:

Dear Elaine,

I wanted to make note of the conversation we had yesterday and let you know the impact that it had on me. Our meeting also left me wondering about all kinds of possibilities that are entering into your life right now.

You said there was a gap opening up between yourself and depression and you had been feeling more yourself in the past week. You noticed that you have played a part in making it much more difficult for depression to mess with your current plans. You have developed a study plan to prepare for the next set of exams and had some study time where depression was only partially present.

It was such a privilege for me when you shared some of your poems and your short story yesterday. I especially loved the story of the six-fingered boy from Badendorp. I couldn't help thinking that the central character in this story reminded me of the kind of courage you have been demonstrating during this very difficult time.

You said that you have claimed back 90% of yourself from depression, which is more than double what you predicted a month ago. I am still trying to figure out how you could reclaim so much of your life back despite the awful power of depression.

I am still mindful of your recognition of the effects of expectation on self and others. That has been a territory that depression loves to travel. How did you challenge the idea that family members can still care for one another without the mother and father having to live under the same roof?

Your words are ringing in my ears:

> "I can accept that I wasn't responsible for Mum and Dad splitting up. They have a right to decide what's best for them and I can decide what's best for me. I'm still allowed to want them back together but I know I can't make that happen. Depression comes in when it tells me that I have the power to change Mum and Dad's mind."

You have noticed also that you are less tired and sleeping easier. I wanted to know more about how you are able to relax and have a clearer mind.

You recognized that recently you are making two steps forward and depression can push you one step back. You sounded very realistic about recognizing that depression is very likely to push in on you still, even though you are on a roll.

Elaine, thank you for sharing your story with me. I can't wait for the next chapter.

With my very warm wishes,
Mary-Anne

A Caution

Because we have laid out a step-by-step guide through the method of narrative counseling, we need to issue a caution about using it. Although this guide is meant to be helpful for counselors beginning to get a handle on a narrative approach to counseling, it can also create distortions. The truth is that very few counseling relationships would ever conform completely to the model we have laid out. Although we recommend this model for learning purposes, we don't recommend slavish adherence to it. Conversations do not follow linear lines of progression. They are messier than that. When it comes to the application of these steps in practice, it may be more useful to think in terms of cyclical progression rather than linear progression. We might therefore find ourselves cycling around these steps many times within a counseling relationship and even within a counseling session. What we can remember is to keep on

■ moving problem stories toward externalized descriptions of problems
■ mapping the effects of externalized problems
■ listening for clues to competence in the midst of problem stories
■ building a story of competence around any instances of it
■ documenting and publicizing achievements

In Chapter 1, we gave you a story to illustrate narrative counseling in action. In this chapter, we have outlined the basic ideas, attitudes, and methods that inform this approach. What we want to convey in this book is all here in nutshell form. What we will go on to do is to elaborate these ideas in several different ways and in relation to some specific challenges that school counselors frequently have placed before them.

3

Reworking Reputations

In this chapter, we look more closely at the work done by language to shape children's experience of school. How people get described is often part of the problem that brings them to counseling. A narrative perspective asks us to think carefully about how words are used and how they operate on us. It also offers us some tools to shift the conversation by speaking a little differently. This chapter will include examples of how to get a purchase on such shifts in order to give young people a say in how they are described and in how they come to think of themselves.

The Discourse of Schooling

Imagine a conversation in the teacher's lounge in which a particular class is being talked about. The class has been providing plenty of challenges for the teacher, and other teachers are supporting her by offering thoughts about what is going wrong. Their talk rapidly moves into a discussion of what is wrong with several individual pupils in the class. Words like *disruptive, disturbed, attention seeking,* and even *attention deficit disordered* are thrown around as explanations for what is happening. The teachers do not want to blame these children unfairly, and there is no shortage of concern for each child's learning needs. Yet despite this concern, they are drawn as if by a magnet into a disparaging way of talking about these children, which they would never do in front of the children or their parents.

The teacher at the center of the conversation feels vaguely dissatisfied with the discussion but cannot specify what disturbs her. She is momentarily overcome by the complex web of meaning that seems to involve the children's disruptive behavior and the teachers' ways of talking about that. It all seems so repetitive and familiar, and yet it doesn't seem to lead anywhere. It certainly doesn't alter the fact that after lunch, she has to go back and manage the same classroom issues. In this chapter, we focus on some aspects of "problematic talk" rather than "problematic people."

Young people encounter in the course of their schooling a range of descriptions of themselves. There are some things said about people in a school that would seldom be heard uttered anywhere else. Take, for example, the way a school report card might describe a young person as "underachieving" or suggest that he "could do better." Or take the way in which a young person who commits misdemeanors against school codes of conduct gets described as "a behavior problem" or "disruptive." The same action on the streets might lead to someone being described as "criminal" or "delinquent."

In other words, there is a definite culture of schooling that has its own distinctive language or discourse. It crosses national and other boundaries and is familiar to everyone who has spent part of his or her life in school. There are, however, many different kinds of talk that take place in schools. School culture features a variety of different genres, or ways of speaking. There is playground banter, classroom interaction, comments that teachers write on students' work, the language of report cards and testimonials, and special education reports. Teachers talk to and about children in stylized ways, in classrooms, to each other in the teacher's lounge, and to parents at parent-teacher meetings. School assemblies and graduation ceremonies also convey descriptions of young people in slightly different genres.

In Chapter 2, we introduced the term *discourse*. "Discourse" is a shorthand term to describe how characteristic ways of speaking develop in particular social contexts. Because schools are distinctive social contexts, it is not surprising that we can talk of school discourse. We are interested in how discourse comes to shape people's thinking and acting and in how taken-for-granted assumptions shape our experience of what happens in schools. Because they are taken for graned, it is hard to notice how these assumptions structure relations between people and even shape the functioning of institutions. For example, behind the description of someone as "gifted," there is a discourse about intelligence that assumes many things about what it means to be called "gifted."

School counselors working in a narrative mode stay alert to the discourses that shape children's experience of school. For example, discourse about race, ethnicity, and culture has a powerful shaping influence on relations within schools. Similarly, gender discourse shapes the differential ways in which girls and boys experience life at school. Yet schools are not just mirrors of the surrounding social world. Schools also have distinctive specialized discourses that underlie pedagogy and institutional structures. One way to notice these discourses at work is to focus on the common ways in which young people are described within the school.

School Descriptions

Let us, for a moment, list some of the descriptions of young people that circulate in schooling discourse. Some of these are related to performance in academic learning tasks in the classroom, such as bright, average, slow; able, exceptional, gifted, intellectually disabled; hardworking, diligent, lazy; nerd, swot, tryhard, top of the class, could do better, underachiever; poor speller, intellectually challenged, honor student, special needs child.

Some are related to the social contexts of young people's lives that they bring with them into the school: delinquent, from the wrong side of the tracks, from a single-parent family, disadvantaged, socially deprived, inner-city kids, at risk, from a dysfunctional family.

Some are related to the specific social world of the classroom or the school: teacher's pet, class clown, truant, troublemaker, bully, behavior problem, disruptive, school refuser, unmotivated, acting out, dropout, attention seeking, discipline problem.

Some relate to social groupings that form in school communities as like-minded young people gather together, often as an expression of disaffection with the social opportunities available to them: skaters, skinheads, druggies, surfies, basers, taggers, gang members, homies.

Some are medical/psychological diagnoses, which increasingly appear in the vocabularies of school personnel: maladjusted, attention deficit disordered, severely emotionally disturbed, dyslexic, conduct disordered, oppositional-defiant, emotionally handicapped, learning disabled.

All of these descriptions involve some kind of evaluation or assessment of the person. In other words, the gaze is at work. Behind each evaluation lies an implicit standard of normality against which the measurement is being made. This standard often remains hidden, but its effects are still felt, particularly by those assessed as abnormal. Because it remains hidden, the cultural and social biases built into accepted standards of normality are seldom open to question.

School counselors have long offered young people some relief from the effects of the gaze by talking to them in "nonjudgmental" ways. In narrative counseling, we are seeking to go one step further. We want to turn the gaze back on itself, so that the hidden standards of normality are themselves open to scrutiny. We want to question both the descriptions that get assigned to individuals and the process of assignation. We ask people to make judgments about the acceptability of these standards of normality, not just about themselves in relation to them.

What Effects Do School Descriptions Have?

You can ask of all such descriptions how accurate they are or how well they mirror the reality of the person they describe. Conventional wisdom would have us place more trust in descriptions that are established with reference to psychological norms based on standardized measures of large populations. This "How accurate?" or "How true?" question is the most common one asked of such ways of speaking.

There is another way of approaching these descriptions, whether they are formal, "scientific" descriptions or informal, lay descriptions. You can bypass the question about how well they mirror reality and ask whether they have real effects. Do these descriptions come to be real through the impact they have in people's lives? Does it make a difference to how a person comes to think of himself and therefore to his life opportunities, to be described in any of these ways?

We believe that words do have effects and that how we speak about ourselves and about others *does* matter. Descriptions, such as the ones we have listed, often have a life of their own, once they have been uttered, that has little to do with the "truth" of the description in the first place. Because children spend a significant part of their early lives at school, we believe that the ways they get described at school are powerfully absorbed into their understandings of themselves and others. They must make sense of their own lives in relation to the way in which they are described by significant others in their school lives.

The Narrative Metaphor

The narrative metaphor helps us see how this happens. Each description can be thought of as a characterization in a story. Characters become caught up in stories that progress through time. Children can be cast as protagonists or supporting characters in a variety of stories according to how they are described. For example, children can be called "underachievers" and then begin to participate in the story of underachievement. They adopt a view of themselves as not quite good enough academically. A teacher might then make a judgment about the reasons for their underachievement, such as "laziness," and begin to treat them more harshly. Resenting the harsher treatment, the children might then become less cooperative with this teacher and produce a lower standard of work. Thus develops a story of "underachievement" not necessarily caused by the events that led to the description in the first place.

Many of the descriptions used in school have very positive effects. From them, young people internalize positive stories of themselves that become long-lasting or even lifelong resources. They come to think of themselves as competent in many ways because they have been described as competent by those who have the power to name. So, they act with confidence and enter with enthusiasm into interactions that recognize and foster their talents and abilities. In such instances, the power of discourse to give shape and form to how we live is not at all oppressive, and those who exercise its naming rights perform desirable social functions.

Counselors, however, often see young people who have encountered descriptions of themselves that are more problematic. These descriptions invite a negative view of self as they are internalized. They specify a role to be played in a very limiting story that is not a base for competence or confidence. Those who have the power to name may play a part in the development of stories of failure or rejection for these people.

In these circumstances, a narrative approach helps a counselor to see each description of a young person as a story about him or her rather than the essential truth about who he or she is. Narrative thinking even takes "scientific" descriptions down off the pedestal of unquestioned truth and treats them as stories, too (Gergen, 1985, 1990; Hoshmand & Polkinghorne, 1992). This does not imply any disrespect for these descriptions. On the contrary, it implies a deep respect for the power and importance of stories. They have significance in all cultures. This includes the cultural traditions that have become embodied in "scientific" rhetoric.

Re-Authoring

The narrative perspective also enables us to see all stories as partial or provisional truths rather than as fixed realities. Stories can be edited and revised. They can be reinterpreted. They can be given new readings or rewritten from a different angle. The work of a counselor can therefore be thought of as helping people in schools become authors of the stories that will shape their lives. Sometimes, this means taking a description thrown up by the discourse of schooling and working to revise this description and the story into which it fits. In the process, counselors first need to help young people separate themselves from the limiting effects of the troubling descriptions and choose self-descriptions through which they would prefer to live.

To accomplish this task, the narrative methods we have outlined in the previous two chapters are very useful. The problematic description can be externalized and spoken about as if it is not the person. For example, Distractions might be named as the problem that comes to visit a particular child in class, whispering in his ear and persuading him to abandon his desire to complete his study tasks. The child might then be invited to evaluate his relationship with Distractions and to fight back against its encroachment into his classroom demeanor. This is very different from an approach that begins with an internalizing description of the problem, such as "poor concentration." It often has much greater appeal to a child. Before elaborating further on this approach, however, let us examine the process by which descriptions of young people in schools come to be fixtures in their identities.

The Power of the Teacher

Not every description comes to be internalized to a degree that it takes up a thematic, organizing function in a person's life. Therefore, we need to think about what might make a particular description meaningful and authoritative. In the relation between a teacher and a pupil, what the teacher says about the pupil carries more weight than what the pupil says about the teacher. The authority that stands behind every utterance by a teacher accrues from the whole history of teacher-pupil relations. It also capitalizes on the knowledge in every pupil's mind that the teacher has the power to direct many day-to-day aspects of a child's life in school. The reverse is not the case. No child has much say in how a teacher's life or career might develop.

Similarly, counselors and psychologists have the power to name and the authority behind their naming rights that makes the descriptions they use hard to ignore. The accumulated knowledge on which their professional role is based lends authority to the descriptions they deploy. Some of the descriptions authorized by this knowledge base lay direct claim to "scientific validity" by appealing to higher standards of objectivity. Once made, such descriptions masquerade as if they are free from social and cultural influences. Therefore, counselors' and teachers' descriptions of young people are hard to resist. The descriptions they use sound incontestable. This authority tends to spread into the descriptions they use without any scientific basis. The knowledge base of a profession therefore constitutes positions of power from which teachers and counselors relate to parents and children.

Such power relations actually contribute to the meanings children take from teachers' words. When a teacher describes a girl as "gifted," for example, this might have a very different impact on that girl's understanding of herself than if a parent uses this description. Now imagine a psychologist who is equipped with professional knowledge about psychological testing making such a description. It carries further weight and authority.

Imagine the possibility of other factors in this girl's life that might also be part of the web of meaning into which the description "gifted" feeds. Classmates may have been teasing her about being a nerd. She may be feeling embarrassed about comparisons being made between her and her siblings. She may be trying hard to gain acceptance to a group of friends and worrying about any description that might mark her as different. She might be anxious about whether she can match the expectations for school success that others might have for her. The word *gifted*, as a result, may have acquired a quite negative set of connotations for her. These negative connotations will play a part in the effects on her of the teacher's description.

An understanding of power relations suggests an ethical care to speak in ways that are neither totalizing nor disrespectful of others. We should never take for granted the effects in another person's life of what we say. This means letting go of the temptation to know best about another person, even when we are invited into such knowing by expectations of us as professionals.

Narrative counseling also aims at a deconstructive conversation (White, 1992) in which we gently subvert dominating patterns of relating and open space for things to change. This is not easy. It is achieved in the first place by adopting a curious attitude.

We might, for example, ask a girl how she came to expect of herself that she would not be good at science, as she is considering her subject choices. We could directly ask whether gender stories that privilege boys' performance in science subjects have influenced her descriptions of herself. We could ask her about the effects of teachers' comments about her science ability on her thinking about herself. Then, we could externalize the stories that have been shaping her preferences and help her separate from them. We can wonder about how things can be otherwise. In this way, we can open up the space for her own preferences to take shape, including her desire to make a small dent in the dominant story of gender-based subject choices. Opportunities to validate an alternative story by significant others in the school can be sought. There may be a teacher who recognizes her talents and abilities and who can be enlisted to support her subject choices.

Deficit Discourse

One of the effects of the development of educational and psychological technologies of evaluation and measurement during the past century has been the increasing precision with which "normality" has been described. However, this precision has had a by-product. It has been accompanied by a proliferation of deficit conditions in psychological discourse (Gergen, 1990, 1994). It is clearly much easier to be assigned a deficit condition than it used to be, simply because there are more such descriptions available to both professionals and laypersons. The coverage of deficit discourse has widened to include much greater proportions of the population. Many of the descriptions listed earlier from school discourse allude to personal deficits (such as maladjusted, remedial reader, behavior problem, underachiever, learning disabled).

"So what is the problem with these deficit descriptions?" you might ask. "Surely, if they describe a problem so that it can be dealt with, that's good, isn't it?"

The answer may be yes, if indeed all such descriptions of deficit did lead to positive changes for people to whom they were applied. The problem is that the easy availability of deficit descriptions directs us to look for pathology rather than for competence or health. Moreover, Gergen has argued that we should take account of the overall effects of deficit descriptions. He lists several pieces of baggage that deficit descriptions bring with them when they come to stay: personal self-enfeeblement, greater reliance on professionals, erosion of community resources. Let us examine each of these pieces of baggage in turn.

Personal Self-Enfeeblement

Deficit descriptions are often taken on board in a totalizing way, as if they touched the essence of a person. Teachers, parents, and children themselves start to assume that a person is, for example, an addictive personality in their very essence, a school refuser by nature, a behaviorally disordered being-to-the-core, an unintelligent person for all time and in all contexts. Thought of in this way, deficit descriptions have a stabilizing effect on people. Like photographic fixing chemicals, they make images of personhood seem more or less permanent. Despite educational and therapeutic efforts to the contrary, deficit descriptions often work to fix a particular understanding of a person. In this way, they work against change.

It is easy to relate to a person described in deficit terms as a tainted person, as someone who is not a fully responsible moral agent. This perspective then invites the person to think of himself as tainted, or less than worthy. Even in his own eyes, his thoughts and feelings require treatment, rather than deserve respect. Rather than an empowering self-belief, personal self-enfeeblement results.

Recently, a counselor who had been trained in narrative therapy was asked by an elementary school principal, "What do you do with a kid who says to you, 'Mrs. Adams, I have had ADHD [attention deficit with hyperactivity disorder] for a few years now. The doctor and Mom and Dad say I will probably have this for the rest of my life, so I have to learn how to adjust to it. You and my teacher will have to adjust to it too! I can't help it that I have ADHD, but I am happy to teach you all about it.' "

Jane, at 10 years old, was speaking as a new recruit to a dominant cultural discourse that emphasizes a deficit condition. Within this discourse, she had come to understand her active demeanor as an immutable biological condition, perhaps one that could only be managed or tamed by chemotherapy. As a result, she and her parents had turned the problem over to an expert authority to manage. She was inviting the school principal to do the same. She should not bother treating Jane as a responsible person. Nor was Jane thinking of herself as a responsible agent. In terms of the interaction between them, a deficit description becomes something of a conversation stopper. It gives no clear guidance about where they can go next, other than place increased faith in a medical solution.

Many people who were significant in Jane's life came to relate to her under the influence of the deficit description. The expert language of the description convinced them of the rightness of the expert's objective analysis. In the face of this expert knowledge, it is easiest to defer. Children, parents, and teachers may all decline to play an active part in the management of the problem. They do not challenge or protest against the problem's effects. Apart from dispensing medication, they become passive onlookers. This was what the school principal was concerned about when she asked the above question of the school counselor. She did not want to be just an onlooker while ADHD ran the show.

Convinced of the rightness of the medicalized description, parents might fail to notice, or register, events or behaviors in the child's life that do not conform to the characteristics of the defined problem.

Medication might be seen as the only solution. Perceivable changes in the problem then get explained as a chemical reaction. Where no apparent change is forthcoming, pessimism and resignation can take hold. When Jane says, "I can't help the way I am or what I do," everyone is invited to lower their expectations about what is possible.

In these ways, the use of deficit language, even when it is designed to help get problems addressed, often hinders what it is designed to achieve. A narrative approach seeks to reverse the deficit logic and to preempt any possibility of self-enfeeblement. Rather, the separation of the person from the problem opens space for people to join forces in effective action rather than in helplessness. Externalizing conversations, by their nature, invite counselors and clients to align themselves on the same side and place the problem on the other side. In such a conversation, ADHD is the problem, Jane is not the problem.

Jane and the counselor, perhaps her parents, and even the principal, can begin to talk about the effect ADHD is having on them all. Is it affecting Jane equally in class, at home, in her sports, at lunchtime, on the playground? What effect does it have on the family? The class? Does it make people (including the principal) feel helpless and frustrated at times? Does it take a break at times? How does it convince Jane that there is nothing she can do about it? Does it also try to convince others that there is nothing they can do about it? How does it become so convincing? Does the medication Jane is taking help her win against ADHD's program for her life? How can school staff join on her side in the battle against ADHD? What have they done so far that is particularly helpful? This is the kind of inquiry that a narrative counselor might instigate as an alternative to the internalizing of deficit thinking.

Reliance on Professionals

Another piece of baggage that comes with deficit logic is greater reliance on professional authority. As we place increased trust in professional knowledge, we decrease accordingly the amount of trust we place in our own competence. In this way, the gap between professionals and laypersons widens, and power relations between professionals and clients are structured. The concern in this is about the proliferation of "progressive infirmity" (Gergen, 1990), the ever-more inclusive reliance on professional treatment or guidance rather than on personal or family resources.

The narrative approach mitigates against this trend by seeking to shift the balance of power in the relationship between counselors and clients. It seeks to include clients, even young children, in decisions about the counseling, rather than assuming professional authority over them. A narrative counselor might ask a young person's permission to ask him or her further questions, for example. The counselor might consult the young person's expert knowledge rather than assuming that all expertise lies in the counselor's head. In other words, he or she might open space for the client to have a say in the counseling process and take a genuine interest in what the client might say to inform the counselor.

Erosion of Local Knowledge

If deficit discourse puffs up the social status of professionals, then it also promotes a complementary erosion of local, commonsense knowledge of how to handle problems. This was evident in the experience of the principal who was feeling helpless in the face of the medicalized description of ADHD. Local, indigenous, or pragmatic ways of handling problems are easily set aside in favor of the more scientific, professional knowledge. In the process, trust in alternative ways of knowing withers, and social networks in which such knowledge has been held shrivel up through underuse. When viewed through a wide-enough lens, the trend is for professional domination to increase at the same time as lay, or local, knowledge is undermined. One aspect of this trend is the ongoing colonization by the privileged discourse of the counselor, teacher, psychologist, or doctor over knowledge shared by members of minority cultural communities.

A narrative counselor seeks to obviate this trend by deliberately searching out local knowledge in the resolution of problems. This search assumes that the solution to any problem already exists in the knowledge of the client and his or her community. The counselor's job is to bring this knowledge out of the shadows and build opportunities for it to be performed. The problem is often not that people do not know how to solve a problem so much as it is that the knowledge of how to solve it is being suppressed, perhaps by the deficit-based description of the problem itself. The counselor needs to stay alert to any shred of an idea or experience that contradicts the rule of a problem in a person's life. When such a moment is discovered, the narrative counselor seeks to build upon it, not by teaching the child skills from her own repertoire, but by mining the vein of knowledge out of which the unique outcome has grown.

Resistance

We are not suggesting that resistance to deficit-based descriptions is uncommon or impossible. People in many situations do fight against the internalization of these descriptions. To be thought of as "cool" among one's friends might often mean maintaining an attitude of indifference to the effects of authoritative descriptions, even in the moment that these effects are impacting on one's life. Or it might mean actively seeking membership in a subgroup that stands defiantly on the fringe of legitimate acceptability, even while it pays the price for social unacceptability.

Even when people come to "realize" the truth of these descriptions, internalize them and accept them as authoritative versions of who they are, it would be a mistake to think that they are happy to see themselves this way. Many will squirm and wriggle and object, even as they are being pinned by the effects of these descriptions. Young people do protest at how they get described by others in school. They may express anger or they may struggle over many years to assert themselves against the effects of others' descriptions.

One 13-year-old young man said to his counselor in a secondary school recently, "I'm ADHD . . . but I don't believe it." This is an interesting statement, if we listen to the contest over meanings it contains. On the one hand, this young man is publicly acknowledging the power and authority of the medical description of himself. He does not say that this is a doctor's or psychologist's opinion of him. He has internalized the meaning of the description to the extent that he says it "is" him. But privately, he still maintains a stance of defiance. Apparently, in some part of himself that professional domination does not enter, he is able to stand back from the process by which socially sanctioned descriptions operate. He keeps for himself the right to believe, or not believe, any particular description. In so doing, he keeps alive a different option for describing himself.

It may be tempting for a counselor to hear, ". . . but I don't believe it," as an example of "denial." Conventional discourse often uses this ploy to disqualify squeals of protest. But this school counselor, thinking in narrative terms, heard two competing stories, one in the voice of legitimate authority and one in the 13-year-old's own voice. She heard him wanting to be a subject in the process of describing, not just an object. She heard him wanting to describe himself in his own terms, not just in someone else's. At times, this can seem like a difficult and seemingly futile act, particularly if no one hears. That the counselor did hear makes it slightly less futile for him to speak his protest. Moreover, the farther she can develop a conversation in which the ripples of this statement flow outward, the more chance he has of developing an identity out of his stance of protest rather than out of the deficit logic.

The Process of Redescription

Let us review the stance we are offering as a template for counselors interested in deploying a narrative method with young people in relation to the descriptions of them that circulate in school discourse. This stance involves hearing all descriptions as products of discourse. This does not mean that these descriptions are wrong or bad; it does mean that we should hear them as culturally produced, partial stories rather than complete and total truths about persons.

The advantage of this perspective is that it enables us to treat with due respect the power of discourses to name people, and then to shape identity and experience through such naming. It also allows us not to get caught by our respect for this process into accepting the inevitability of the descriptions and their effects. As we convey this attitude to young people, we can open up enough space for them to contest these descriptions in their deeds as well as in their words and to shape their own identities deliberately.

Narrative counseling begins with separating the person from the problem. The internalizing descriptions themselves are all candidates for speaking about in an externalizing way. Rather than believing that Rowena is a school refuser, we can ask how Staying-Away-From-School has been persuading her each morning out of going to class. Instead of joining in the description of Carlos as learning disabled, we can inquire about the effects of a "learning-disabled lifestyle" (Stewart & Nodrick, 1990) on everyone's expectations of Carlos (including his own). Instead of asking teachers to make allowances for Gabrielle because she is "emotionally disturbed," we can explore the things that are undermining her emotional equilibrium and ask teachers to support the things she is doing to struggle against these. We can engage Damien in a review of a "druggie" or "skater" lifestyle and an examination of its effects (positive and negative) on his school career. We can invite Karena to describe and name the discourse that unfairly leaves her with the description of "slut" after she was raped at a party by three boys. We can ask Simon whether the reputation "disruptive" that has been shaping teachers' responses to him fits his picture of himself.

These types of questions can then be followed by an exploration of the ways in which each of these people would prefer to describe him- or herself. Preferable descriptions can be anchored back to events that illustrate them and people who recognize them. A different description, which connects with an alternative story, can be built up and fleshed out. The two descriptions can be pitted in competition with each other, and the counselor and client can apply their combined weight behind the cause of advancing the more favorable description.

This process of redescription is the point of this chapter. Our purpose in taking time to examine the ways in which dominant discourses work people over has been to reach the point of departure that redescription offers. The methods of working that we illustrated in Chapter 1 and spelled out in Chapter 2 are the tools in this process. In the next chapter, we take this process of redescription into a particular area of concern for school counselors: how to work with young people who are in trouble with school authorities.

4

Conversations With Kids
Who Are "In Trouble"

In many schools, the counselor is expected to help young people who are "in trouble" with teachers or school administrators to make changes to disruptive, illegal, or abusive patterns of behavior. Being in trouble with school authorities makes for a strong likelihood that a young person is going to attract the kind of totalizing, deficit description that we talked about in Chapter 3.

How, then, can counselors engage with young people who are in trouble? How can they provide them with challenges that will help them make changes to their behavior, and still treat them with respect, rather than colonize them against their will as objects of punishment or behavior modification? This is not a task for which traditional approaches to counseling equip counselors very well.

Client-centered listening, for example, is not likely on its own to be effective in producing enough leverage for change, even if it establishes a strong relationship with troubled young people. Psychodynamic approaches are not speedy enough in producing change in often volatile situations. Approaches that rely on cathartic expressions of feeling may sometimes inadvertently support behavior that is abusive of others.

We believe a narrative approach does offer some fresh perspectives for school counselors who are willing to pick up this responsibility. The freshness lies in the distinctive conversational style that young people experience as calling forth their best selves, rather than dwelling on, or disparaging, their worst selves. Moreover, the externalizing conversation of a narrative interview allows the bypassing of guilt and shame and moves more directly toward acting responsibly. In this chapter, we apply the narrative thinking we have been outlining to a range of typical "troubles" that can bedevil young people's school careers and show how it can produce often surprisingly rapid and effective change.

Stealing Trouble

Jason was in trouble often at school and in the community. He had developed a habit of stealing and had been caught red-handed several times at school. Each time, the seriousness with which the misdemeanors were regarded increased. On the last occasion, he had been temporarily suspended from school and readmitted on a "last chance" basis. He was also well known to the local police for petty theft incidents in the community. It seemed that he was well and truly launched on a career of crime. He was referred to the school counselor "as a last resort" to see if she could help him with the stealing problem.

It was clear that the usual disciplines employed within schools were not succeeding in internalizing honesty in Jason. For many young people, they do quite successfully achieve this purpose. This is not usually done by any kind of repression. Punishment is not necessary for most young people in order to train them in honesty. Rather, the ethics of living in a community and respecting other people's property is trained into people over a number of years by family, school, community, and media narratives. The stories of respect for property and for other people are told often, and practices that embody such stories are demonstrated, rehearsed, and rewarded. In the process, children grow to understand themselves as characters in such stories. They learn the practices of honesty and adopt the identities that go with these practices. As they identi*fy,* they construct identi*ty*.

What we are referring to here is the kind of discipline that is not aimed at repressing any natural impulses in children. Rather, it is embodied in the many daily interactions that serve to constitute identity. It is formative rather than repressive. What it forms will eventually become their social impulses. In school, it is achieved in the everyday relational practices between children and teachers. From the first days of school, attitudes toward school property are shaped, beginning with the assigning of spaces (desks, lockers, hooks on which to hang schoolbags) that are under the individual's control. Children also witness, or are told stories about, the consequences of crossing the boundaries into criminal behavior.

However, these dominant stories, though they are powerful and influential in most children's lives, are never completely dominant. Their influence is not universal. Stories of honesty are not equally influential in constituting identities in children. Some children, like Jason, learn to steal. How do we account for this? Perhaps there are competing stories in people's lives. Perhaps people who are positioned outside the social privileges and advantages in the school or the community do not see the dominant stories as relevant to their own lives. Social marginalization (Jason was from a poor, Maori family) weakens the influence of mainstream stories. Conventional stories about honesty also require some dishonest identities, which can serve as salutary examples to those who are within the mainstream. Powerful social discourses define narrow little places within which some people live. For example, some people grow up defining themselves as "criminal" by nature, although this description is seldom entirely of their own making.

Jason's counselor had a choice. She could have worked with Jason to reproduce himself exactly in the mold prescribed by the authorities in the school and community. This may have required Jason to think of himself as in deficit. The desire to steal could be explained to Jason (and thus his identity imputed to him) as the result of a moral deficit ("You're a bad person"), or a medical deficit ("You've got a conduct disorder"), or a social skill deficit ("You have poor impulse control").

However, Maria, Jason's counselor, had been trained to think in narrative ways. Instead of thinking of stealing as an aspect of Jason, she talked to him about it as an influential story in the world around him. She externalized stealing. She invited him to talk about his relationship with Stealing, and to examine its effects in his life. She asked him to evaluate these effects and weigh up whether they were things he wanted to happen to him. She didn't blame him for Stealing having this influence, but she also did not try to excuse his actions. She asked him questions like:

- How did you get signed up on Stealing's team?
- With what did Stealing promise you or entice you into its influence?
- How does Stealing get other people to think about you?
- How does it get you to think about yourself?
- What effects is Stealing having in your life right now? Is this what you want?

Jason made it clear that he did prefer to think of himself as an honest person. He did want other people to trust him. He didn't like the reputation he had acquired. Did this make him a hypocrite? Perhaps, but such a view of him would ignore the struggle going on in Jason. Human beings are seldom totally consistent in their behavior. Anyone who has ever felt torn between two thoughts knows what it is like to have competing stories clamoring for attention. Jason had stories of honesty and trustworthiness on the one hand, and stealing on the other, competing for his allegiance. Because Maria recognized him as a person in the middle of such a struggle, he was positioned as responsible for his response in a way that he would not have been had she seen him through the lens of a totalizing description (e.g., criminal by nature). Totalizing descriptions offer little but the chance to submit or react.

As a result, Jason committed himself to re-authoring his identity in a way that did not feature stealing. This meant more than just stopping the behavior of stealing. He could and did do that. His identity, however, was not completely under his control. It existed in the descriptions that circulated in conversations around him as much as it did in his inner conversations. Jason discovered this when he began to make changes for himself. The story of stealing continued to make its presence felt even after he had decided not to be persuaded by it. Friends still asked him to steal things for them. His family still suspected him of stealing some money that had gone missing at home. Teachers were still looking at him suspiciously and waiting to pounce if he did anything wrong. If something went missing at school, his bag would be searched. The identity of "thief" still featured in others' versions of who he was.

For this reason, a narrative counselor needs to work with the social context of identity change as much as with the internal commitments someone like Jason is making. If conversations with the counselor were important steps in the re-authoring of Jason's identity (which they were), then it became important to involve other people in noticing and crediting the changes as well. To his credit, Jason knew this. He asked Maria in two successive counseling meetings whether the school principal had noticed that his "name had not been coming up" in relation to disciplinary matters. Of course, busy school principals seldom pay a lot of heed to the many names that are *not* coming to their attention, so Jason's concern about this point was wise. A narrative counselor assisting a young person to make good his escape from trouble does well to follow his wisdom.

Trouble in the Classroom

Sometimes, matters referred to a school counselor may have to do with troublesome behavior in the classroom. Usually, such concern is expressed by teachers, who want the counselor to "fix" the student. A counselor has to tread carefully here. Counseling can appear to be a simple extension of repressive disciplinary procedures. If used simply to bring people into line, it can inadvertently support social control mechanisms, bolster social hierarchies, obscure power relations, and reproduce various forms of social marginalization. These functions are in opposition to the goals of narrative therapy. At the same time, narrative concerns about power relations do not imply that irresponsible behavior should be smiled upon with liberal tolerance as an understandable result of the operation of power.

The challenge is to engage a young person who has been behaving disruptively in a classroom in a productive and yet respectful conversation, which opens doors to change. Real, transformative change will both please the teacher and allow the young person to exercise her own voice. Here are some of the principles and strategies that can be borne in mind by a narrative counselor:

- Treat the young person as a responsible human being whose actions make sense to her.
- Be curious about the young person's thoughts about the issue and indicate that you do regard his viewpoint as important.
- Distinguish between the intentions behind a behavior and its effects.
- Decline the invitation to advocate for the authoritative perspective of the school administrators and teachers.
- Decline also the invitation to advocate for the young person as a poor, misunderstood victim.
- Invite the young person to make meaning for herself about the messages of concern or anger expressed by teachers.
- Talk about the issue in an externalizing way (e.g., as Trouble or Tantrums or Disruptive Behavior) and avoid language that attributes the problem to individual characteristics or deficiencies.
- Inquire about the history of events that have led to the current concerns.
- Inquire about the influence of dominant discourses about gender, race, and class on the externalized situation.
- Invite the young person to express her preferences for responsible, nondisruptive behavior without implying any criticism for hypocrisy if her behavior does not closely match her words.

- Ask the young person to evaluate the current state of relations between himself and his teacher and whether this is satisfactory for him. This can include asking about the trajectory of current developments and where they are likely to lead if left unchecked.

- Ask questions to open up new possibilities in a way that assumes the young person to be exercising some agency in the design of her relationship with class teachers.

- Mediate between the young person and the teacher in order to stimulate an ongoing conversation about the kind of relationship that would be pleasing to both of them.

Here are some examples of some questions (each representing a line of inquiry) that might be asked in such conversations:

- Is the situation between you and your teacher troubling you as well the teacher? How so? What do the teacher's concerns mean to you?

- When did this Trouble first enter the classroom?

- What does Trouble have you doing? How does it get the teacher to respond to you? For example, does it get teachers to monitor you closely and always expect you to be doing something wrong?

- What sort of reputation does Trouble seem to want for you? Is this a reputation with which you are comfortable?

- If you were to set out to shock the teacher out of the bad reputation she seems to be attached to for you, what would you have to do more of?

- What sort of relationship with teachers do you most enjoy? Have there been any occasions when things were like that with this teacher, even for a few minutes on one day? What were you both doing to produce this?

- Does your behavior in some way serve as a protest against some injustice or unfairness that concerns you? Have you always had this sense of justice? Is it important to you? Have you ever found ways to express your sense of justice in ways that don't upset your own reputation with the teacher?

"Who the Hell Are You?"

Marcus had been referred to the counselor by his science teacher. The referral included a series of descriptions of Marcus's nature and his internal motivations, which seemed to the teacher to describe the problem. Words used were *belligerent, talking back, reluctant to get to work, talking with neighbors, stirring.* Such descriptions certainly amounted to an unenviable reputation, which had Marcus attracting the attention of the school disciplinary authorities.

Donald, the school counselor, spoke to Marcus about the development of this reputation without ascribing its origins to internal motivations in him. These descriptions were instead spoken about in an externalizing way. Their influence in his life was discussed. He was asked to evaluate these descriptions. As a result, Marcus was able to separate himself from these descriptions just a little bit. From this position, he could be asked to speculate on the process by which such descriptions managed to stick to him. In the process, he noticed his reactions to people who imposed on him in any way, either at school or at home. His protests against such impositions were often expressed in the tone of, "Who the hell are you?" he explained. Marcus and Donald in fact began to use Who-the-hell-are-you? as a name for the problem. However, Marcus did not like the effects of Who-the-hell-are-you? in his school life. Trouble with his science teacher was not what he wanted at all.

Donald inquired about the presence of other descriptions of Marcus in other areas of his life. This began a process of undermining the influence of Who-the-hell-are-you? Marcus spoke about the reputation he had as a baby-sitter. In this context, people knew him as a *worker* and used words like *reliable, patient, dependable, honest, efficient,* and *quiet* to describe him. The contrast between these two sets of descriptions was sharp.

Donald was interested in how strong each of these descriptions was. How much of Marcus's life did each of them occupy? Marcus weighed them up and reported that there was a fifty-fifty split between the two identities. However, he was also clear that he preferred the Worker description, and this was the one he would most like to stick in other people's minds about him, especially at school. Together, Marcus and Donald set up an experiment to see if the preferable Worker description could become more present at school. Marcus could not achieve this on his own. Reputations are not the sole property of the person to whom they attach themselves. The challenge was to open up space for the Worker description to take root in the perceptions of teachers and classmates.

Donald was now conversationally aligned with Marcus, on his side, against the problem of Who-the-hell-are-you? If others could be enlisted on this same side against the problem, then there was a chance that a new reputation might be crafted. So, they worked together to decide whom to advise of the developments they were plotting. In the end, two teachers were chosen as most likely to notice the Worker description in class. These teachers were primed by Donald, with Marcus's connivance, to look for signs of the Worker in class. In particular, they were asked to interpret his putting up his hand in class as a request for help, rather than as a disruption.

A week later, Donald asked Marcus about the extent of the influence of the Worker during the week. Marcus was pleased to report that the Worker had accounted for 95% of his time in class during this week. Donald expressed surprise and asked Marcus how he had done it. Marcus had to think hard to explain what he had done, but Donald persisted with the question. Marcus came up with four things that had contributed to the success. He listed these as not talking, being quick, being tidy, and not attracting attention.

Donald then invited Marcus to look into the future. He wondered out loud about what ongoing effects this trend could have. In 2 weeks' time, if they were to look back and see that the Worker had been the main description of his classroom demeanor, what possible effects might this have in his life? Donald noted down Marcus's predictions. He then took out an envelope and put the future predictions inside and sealed the envelope. They agreed to open this envelope at a later date and compare the predictions with what transpired.

Two weeks later, Donald spoke to the teacher who had first referred Marcus. This time, the teacher was more than just pleased. He described Marcus in very different terms. He said that Marcus had "excelled by a hundred and fifty percent" in his work in class.

Documenting Progress

With another student who came to him dragging a fearsome classroom reputation featuring trouble of many kinds, Donald also worked to produce a document that spoke of the realigned relationship with trouble that they crafted. On this occasion, they decided on a letter to all of Darren's teachers announcing his intention to separate himself from Trouble and to forge a new reputation. The letter also served the purpose of alerting the teachers to look for signs of this new development. The letter went like this:

April 10

Most excellent teachers of Darren Jakich:

Darren realizes that he has a reputation with his teachers that includes words like:

> had problems
> attitude problem
> better when he's away
> disturbing
> disruptive
> struggling
> can do work sometimes
> needs watching
> backchat
> rude

Darren realizes that this reputation is ripping him off.

HE WANTS TO CHANGE IT!!!

TO: WORKING BETTER
      IMPROVING
      NOT GETTING INTO TROUBLE

Darren is going to try to change his reputation with you.

Darren does not ask for special treatment but he does ask that you (please) NOTICE HIS EFFORTS TO CHANGE HIS REPUTATION.

Thank you for helping Darren with this. We wish him the best of luck.

Kind regards,

Donald M.

Combating Abusive Behavior

Much disruptive behavior that comes to the attention of teachers and school administrators has to do with events in the relations between teachers and pupils. These are the events that potentially interfere with teachers' ability to do their jobs. Often, less attention is paid to interference with children's learning that does not directly involve teachers. We are referring here to the things that happen between children in a classroom or around the school. Quite abusive behaviors can take place between young people that teachers are but dimly aware of. These may involve ongoing bullying or harassment, mocking and teasing those who are different from the majority in some way, sexist or heterosexist putdowns, racial conflicts, outbreaks of violence, or damage to other children's property.

School counselors can become aware of such incidents taking place around the school. Although the temptation may be for counselors to focus their energy on the weightier family problems presented to them or on the educational counseling requiring attention, harassing or violent behavior among pupils in school should not be overlooked. In their interactions with each other, young people are shaping and honing their relational skills, their identities, and their patterns of response to many situations they will encounter in their lives. A pattern of sexist putdowns and mildly harassing behavior toward girls at 13 years old may lead a boy down a path toward a controlling or violent behavior pattern in a marriage 15 years later. Similarly, the development of an alternative story about relations between men and women at age 13 can develop into a respectful and equitable relationship pattern in adulthood.

For the recipients of abusive behavior, counseling can focus on the ways in which power gets constituted in such relations and its effects. Counselors can help children and young people to notice the internalizing effects of abusive behavior—how it undermines confidence and becomes entwined with guilt, fear, and self-blame. Then, counseling can focus on restorying the identities and relationships in ways that do not leave people trapped in victimhood and that do encourage them to have a voice in the kind of relations they would like to see develop in their lives.

With the perpetrators of abusive behavior, a different kind of approach is needed. From a narrative perspective, there is much to be learned from the work of Alan Jenkins (1990) with adult perpetrators of violent or abusive behavior. We would advocate using similar principles with young people who are beginning to engage in the patterns of behavior that lead to full-blown violent and abusive relations later in life.

Such counseling is clearly "disciplinary" in nature, because it is intended to train children in identities and relations that are free from abuse and violence. In our view, though, all conversations are productive or reproductive of discourse and, in the end, of identity and relations. In other words, it is in the conversations and interactions of our lives that we discipline ourselves and each other to be the kinds of people we become. The crucial question is about the nature of what we are being disciplined to become. What kind of relations are being forged? Whose interests are served or whose obscured by this way of speaking? Whose voice is made possible and whose silenced or marginalized? Who is being held accountable to whom?

Jenkins emphasizes three principles for the engagement of people in a process of changing their abusive behavior:

- Declining invitations to attribute responsibility for violence to factors beyond the person's influence.
- Inviting the person to challenge any restraints to acceptance of responsibility for his own actions.
- Acknowledging and highlighting each and every scrap of evidence of the person's acceptance of responsibility for his actions.

These principles can then be elaborated into a series of what Jenkins calls "invitations" to responsibility. Such invitations are questions that call forth answers in sequential steps toward abandoning abusive behavior. Instead, they invite the development of an identity and a reputation based on more respect for others. We outline the steps in the sequence of invitations.

Inviting the young person to address his violence or abuse

The counselor asks if the young person can "help me understand" the events that led to coming to counseling. In the process, the counselor avoids any talk about the reasons for the violence, or any blaming of other people for it. Attendance at the counseling session is treated as a significant step from the start. Rather than allowing this step to be brushed off with a comment like, "I was told to come," the counselor can inquire about the meaning of the young person's attendance at counseling to face up to such a difficult issue, even when he was told to come.

For example:

- It must have taken a lot of courage to come through the door.
- A lot of people deeply regret hurting other people but find it too difficult to face up to what they have done. How come you are managing to do that?
- What does it say about you that you can start to do that?

A person can also be asked to enter directly into such courage by answering questions like:

- Can you handle talking about your violence?

or

- Are you strong enough to face up to what you have done?

Inviting the young person to argue for respectful,
nonabusive ways of relating

If he shows any sense of being unhappy about his own abusive actions, he can be asked to describe how he would like to act in his best intentions. For example:

- What are your beliefs about how you should behave toward girls?
- What sort of friendships do you most value?

■ What sort of relationship would you ideally most like to have with this person?

■ Do you want other people to feel frightened of you? If not, how would you prefer others to feel toward you? What kind of relationship would you need to have with them for them to feel that way?

Often though, such a person might seek to blame the other person for his own abusive behavior.

■ She gave me cheek.

■ He was hassling me.

This can be responded to in the following way:

■ Did this really upset you?

■ What does it say about the kind of relationships you would like to have with others around school that you were upset by this?

■ So, tell me about the ideal kinds of friendly relations you would prefer to have?

Once the client has made a statement about his belief in, or preference for, respectful, mutual, friendly relations with others (no matter how contradictory to the recent behavior), he can be asked to elaborate on this statement in the following ways:

■ You seem to be telling me that you would prefer relationships that are free from violence/threats/harassment (or whatever the problem might be described as). Is that right?

■ Can you help me understand how you came to this decision?

■ Is this a new idea for you, or have you thought about this for a long time?

■ Would you like to have friendships or relationships without resorting to violence/harassment yourself? Why?

■ Would you like to be able to refrain from violence/harassment even when the other person is being quite unreasonable?

*Invite the young person to examine his misguided efforts
to develop responsibility*

In this step, the discrepancy between stated intentions and ideals and what has actually happened can be examined. This is not done in a spirit of proving the ideals and better intentions wrong in light of the evidence to the contrary. Rather, these are retained as desired ways of being that are currently being restrained or interfered with. Things are getting in the way: things like violence, being intoxicated by outrage at how he was being treated, cultural stories about not being a wimp or not taking no for an answer, incitements from others, reputation with his buddies, and so on. The violence or harassing behavior can then be examined in detail—how it happened, what led up to it, what effect it had on each of the people involved.

This kind of conversation can be opened up in the following manner:

- I now understand that you don't want to hurt other people and that you would like to have friendships and relationships that are free from violence or harassment. You have made it clear how important these things are to you. What I don't yet understand is what has stopped you from always sticking to these principles.
- Do you think it would be helpful if you understood what has interfered with you achieving a violence- or harassment-free life?
- How would this be helpful?

Invite the young person to identify time trends in behavior

The focus here is on the trajectories along which violence or harassment might take a person. A counselor can invite a young person to stand back from the present moment in time and see the bigger picture. The past and the present can be used as reference points for asking about the future. The question is whether things are getting better or worse. Is the relationship between this person and the recipient of his violence improving or deteriorating? What effect is violence/harassment having on his reputation in the school? Is it growing or diminishing? The future can then be introduced as an imagined reference point. The counselor can ask the young person, "If things were to keep on getting worse, where could they end up?"

This kind of question can lead to a new awareness of the social consequences of a general trend in behavior rather than an immediate focus on the current situation. It can be enough to lead to a reevaluation of the trajectory. In fact, a counselor can actually ask for this reevaluation:

- Is this the direction you want things to go?
- Why not?

Externalize the restraints to respectful behavior

At this point, the counselor can work with the student to externalize the restraints to respectful behavior. It is important that these restraints are not spoken of as causes of, or excuses for, abusive behavior. Such talk can lead to an inadvertent justification for unacceptable abuses because they seem to be explainable, almost inevitable.

A young person can conclude, "It's not my fault that I was so violent. It's because I had such a lousy upbringing myself and I've just never had a chance in life. Why doesn't everyone feel sorry for me?" This is not a position from which to learn to take responsibility.

The narrative perspective is subtly different and needs to be carefully distinguished. A lousy upbringing and being the recipient of violence and abuse may lead to any number of life patterns. None of them is determined by past events. In every interaction with others, we exchange communications that call forth from each other recursive patterns of behavior that are echoes from our past. However, we also draw from current cultural influences in the world around us. Living in a world of macho aggression and competition, for example, might restrain a young man from developing caring and peaceful qualities, or from rejecting the models of abuse shown to him in childhood. But just as surely, associating with people who appreciate caring and respectful behavior might restrain past abusive experiences from influencing a person's behavior. Therefore, it is just as important to identify and separate from current restraints on change as it is to make links back to past events or "causal factors" that make change difficult (Bateson, 1972).

In fact, people make changes all the time. A counselor's job is to facilitate the intentional choice that can be exercised in change processes. From a narrative perspective, it is more useful to ask questions about *what is stopping desired change from happening* than it is to ask *what is causing the things that need to be changed*. The difference lies in the possibility for the generation of hope. Analyzing causal factors can make problems appear overwhelmingly difficult to change. Assuming the possibility of change and analyzing the obstacles that need to be dealt with engenders much more optimism and undermines the power of problems.

Here are some examples of the kinds of questions that can be asked to make restraints on change visible:

- What has stopped you so far from taking responsibility for violent behavior?
- What sorts of things might make this seem difficult?
- Who or what would support you in not facing up to violence?
- Are there any things that people can say or do that actually lead you away from your desire to respect other people?
- Does macho talk, or street culture, or gang loyalty, or racism, or alcohol or drug use make it easier for you to give in to violence or easier for you to stand up against violence? Why is that?

Once a piece of discourse that is restraining more responsible behavior is named, it can be externalized and spoken of as separate from the person. For example, patriarchal ideas about women can influence a young man's disrespectful attitude toward a woman teacher or underlie sexual harassment of female classmates. In an externalizing conversation about such a problem, Patriarchal Ideas might be represented as tricking him out of the more respectful and friendly relationships with women that he would prefer to have. He is able to save some face by blaming Patriarchal Ideas and, in so doing, to begin to separate himself from them.

If the counselor persists at this point in asking him about the recipe that these Patriarchal Ideas might have for his relationships with women (a recipe that he is saying he rejects), he then might take further steps to reject the influence of this recipe in his life. This process can be furthered by asking *mapping-the-influence questions*. For example:

1. How have these Patriarchal Ideas had an influence in your life? What have they talked you into? What plans do they have for your life? What sort of relationships do they stand for? What kind of person do they try to persuade you to be? How much influence do they have over you?

2. How have you influenced the progress of Patriarchal Ideas in your life? How have you distanced yourself on any occasion you can think of from the demands of patriarchal thinking? Have you noticed any times when you have stood up to these ideas and thought more for yourself? Have you ever accepted a rejection from a woman without trying to bully or harass her to change her mind? How did you do that? What does this say about you?

Deliver irresistible invitations to challenge restraints

Now that a basis has been established for talking about the abusive behavior in a way that separates the person from the problem, we are in a position to issue some clear challenges to act more responsibly. Alan Jenkins (1990) calls these challenges "irresistible invitations." They are designed to sharpen commitment to more responsible and respectful behavior and to prepare the way for significant change, rather than leaving responsibility for change in the hands of good intentions. These invitations are carefully constructed questions that can be put in the form of limited choices. A school counselor might need to take some time with a client to explore such a question until it has been fully answered.

Here are some examples of the questions that might be asked:

■ Can you handle the job of controlling your own violence, or would you prefer the school to take over controlling it for you?

- Are you willing to take responsibility for your abusive behavior, or would you prefer to keep on asking others to take responsibility by blaming them?

- Does complaining about how you were provoked really help you act in the responsible way you have been arguing for, or does it give you an excuse for being abusive?

- Could you handle relationships with female teachers in which you were required to show respect and courtesy, or is that too much for you?

- Are you willing to stand up to feelings of insecurity and fear when a girl chooses to reject you or wants to do things her own way rather than your way?

- Can you handle a school in which girls are given equal opportunities as boys, or do you need girls to prop up male egos by always taking a backseat?

- Is it important to you to earn back the respect of your teachers/friends, or do you think they should give it to you out of right? How important is that to you?

- Would you want this respect to be genuine respect, or would you settle for a pretense, such as their saying what they think you want to hear?

- Are you ready to take action on this issue, or do you need more time to get up the courage?

At this point, the counselor can respond to any positive statements by the student with some caution. This does not mean that the counselor should communicate a disrespectful doubt, but there is a responsibility to test the sincerity of assertions by asking questions like:

- Are you sure about this?

- Have you thought through the consequences of making this decision?

- How can you prove to yourself that you are ready to make these changes?

- What makes you think you are ready?

- Can you help me understand how it is that you are ready?
- Old habits die hard, you know. Have you thought about that?
- Are you prepared to accept that for some time, other people will not believe that you have changed?

The aim of these questions is for the student to hear himself say out loud the arguments for the changes he is considering. This is more persuasive than anything the counselor might say to support the intention to change.

Facilitate taking action

If the buildup to this point has been careful enough, we are now at a point where meaningful change can be planned. We are looking here for real and demonstrable change, not just vague commitments to *"not hit her again."* This kind of commitment is so passive that it is unlikely to be worth much when it is tested under pressure. What is needed is a careful planning of the detail of the action that will be taken. This may include:

- the self-talk that may need to take place
- the choice of responses in specific situations
- the preparation and rehearsal necessary to make these responses
- the active construction of alternative ways of relating to others
- the possible supports or allies that might be enlisted to make this response viable

Here are some questions that can open up the necessary conversation for these developments to happen:

- What would you need to do to get violence out of your relationships?
- How could you prove to your teachers and friends that you are committed to nonabusive behavior in class?
- What strategies can you think of to put your intentions into action?

▓ What signs will you look for to know whether your strategies are working?

▓ How could you demonstrate to your girlfriend that you respect her feelings and wishes, even when they differ from yours?

▓ How could you show to other people that you want them to feel safe around you?

▓ How would you know if someone was still feeling scared of you? What could you do to reassure her that she is safe?

▓ What would you need to do to prove that you are not a slave to angry feelings?

▓ How could you convince the teachers that they don't need to be so vigilant in watching your every move?

▓ What would you need to do to convince yourself and the school board that you were taking full responsibility for your past behavior?

It is important to note that these questions are intended as openings to a conversation. Curiosity then needs to direct the counselor's attention to the careful and detailed exploration of answers to these questions. Ideas that the person comes up with need to be grounded in experience by asking for examples of the idea in practice. Moreover, the history of each idea can be traced through asking about:

▓ where it came from

▓ who might have had an influence on such thinking

▓ what models might be around to draw from

Then, in follow-up meetings, the development of these strategies in practice needs to be traced. The counselor's task becomes one of inviting the development of a story of what has taken place. Two types of questions are recommended for this process:

▓ What have you been doing to take back your life from abusive relationships?

▓ What does it mean that you have taken those steps?

The first question is about events that have happened on "the landscape of action" (White, 1992). A typical response at a follow-up meeting can be, "Not much." Counselors should not be deterred from asking further questions at this point. Problem stories are likely to continue to exert their dominance in ways that make it hard for people to notice changes. Small changes often seem too insignificant to report. However, small, insignificant changes are often the first steps in the construction of larger changes. Therefore, the counselor should seek out even minute developments and amplify their significance, rather than let them slide farther into insignificance. Of particular value is for the counselor to ask *how* the client achieved even the tiniest of moves against the problem.

The second question is about how people make meaning of events. This has been called "the landscape of meaning" (White, 1995). Stories that have significance in people's lives need to develop a thematic coherence. Therefore, a narrative that is begun in terms of actions can be developed by exploring the *significance* of each little action. Questions that can stimulate this kind of story development express curiosity about:

- What a person said to himself about what he did
- Feedback from others about what she did
- What this step tells him about himself
- The personal qualities shown by her action and the history of these qualities
- The extent of influence on the problem that his action represents
- The encouragement that can be drawn from her achievement for future actions.

Apologies

One specific possible strategy at this stage is that the person may be prepared to make some apologies for past abusive actions. As acknowledgments of past wrongs toward others and as commitments to change, such statements may have enormous value. They can make a considerable difference for those who have been wronged and can serve as a turning point toward a different relationship in the future.

There are also some dangers with apologies. They can create an inflated expectation of change on either side. For the person who makes the apology, there is the danger that he or she may think that the concern is concluded at this point. However, one moment of acknowledgment is not the same thing as a change in a relationship. In narrative terms, one plot element does not make a story. It needs to be linked to other events to constitute a plot that moves through time. For the person who receives the apology, there is the danger of expecting that a single moment of apology will change things forever, as well as the opposite danger of cynically thinking that an apology is worth nothing at all.

From a narrative perspective, we would be concerned to give an apology a chance. We would also caution against thinking of an apology, no matter how sincere, as sufficient for producing substantive change. The key to change is weaving the apology into a larger story. This might require asking questions that encourage ripples from the apology to spread. Here are some examples of such questions:

- What does it take for you to apologize like that?
- What does it mean to you to hear him apologize like that?
- Is this a new event, or has it happened before?
- Is this apology based on an understanding of how you hurt the other person? What have you understood about how she was affected by what you did?
- What are you doing to demonstrate the sincerity of your apology?
- How would you know that her apology was meant?
- How long would you need these changes to continue in order to be able to trust them?

Truancy Trouble

Another form of trouble that can dog a person's school career and become a compelling habit is truancy. In various cultural contexts, skipping out of school can be given a variety of exotic labels. In New Zealand colloquial lingo, it is often called "wagging." Wagging rapidly becomes attached to the reputation of the person who is caught skipping class. School officials and teachers come to know a student as a "truant," and classmates activate the reputation of "wagger" to describe the person.

From the moment such a description gets applied, a reputation begins to form, and the young person is required to negotiate his or her identity in relation to it. As with some other reputations in schools, this one seems to catch and stick like wool to Velcro. Young people often complain of the difficulty of shedding a reputation for truancy.

"I come to class every day for weeks on end and nobody notices, and then I take one day off and everyone's on my back. Suddenly I'm a wagger again."

From a narrative perspective, this cry of anguish has a point. The reputation of "being" a wagger is a story about the person based on a selection of events. As a description, it is a totalizing description. It sums up the person. In doing so, it overlooks all contrary evidence, as any summary must. The many occasions on which the person comes to school and attends class are factored out of the equation that produces the description. Such is the nature of stories.

From a narrative perspective, we are interested in recovering some of the experiences that are left out of the accepted story about a person. This interest is not just out of concern for a more correct picture of how things really are. It is also out of concern for how things can be otherwise, a concern for new possibilities. Therefore, when someone has been truant, a narrative counselor might not just be interested in what had caused the truancy, but also in how the student had overcome the truancy habit in order to be at school today. Questions might be asked along the lines of:

- What helped you to say no to wagging today?
- What did you say to yourself to persuade yourself to come?
- Did you think about anything in some new way?
- What does it mean that you are here today? Does it say anything about your desire to reject the influence of wagging in your life?
- Where does this desire come from?
- Who or what supports this desire in you?

Maria had been captured by the "wagging habit." She had been involved with a group of friends who felt alienated from school. With the help of her counselor, Aileen, she began to fight back against wagging and to reinvest in her own future. As Maria started to succeed in reclaiming her school career from wagging, Aileen consulted with her about how she was achieving this.

She asked about the news from teachers that Maria was doing really well.

Maria replied, "Oh, I just sat down and thought to myself about what I wanted to do when I left school. I was thinking, well, what can I do, what can I do?"

Sensing the start of a story, Aileen sought to take up the role of scribe to Maria's knowledge. "Can I write some of this down, because I guess I'm interested for when I have someone who's into the wagging habit. Is it OK if I say to someone, well, I know there was this student who beat the wagging habit, and these were some of the things that were helpful to her. Is that all right?"

"Yeah, that's OK. They'll probably go, oh, that must be Maria, because when I used to wag, I used to see people up there [at the shops], and now they come up to me and say, 'You gonna wag?' and I say, 'No, I'm going to class.' And they go, 'Oh, you goin' to class, I'll go too.' "

Maria continues to describe how she has been making choices to spend more of her time with friends who are supportive of her going to class. She reassesses the past 3 years of her schooling with the comment, "I made one path, and when I look back on it, it was just for me to fail. Like, that's how I looked at myself. I can't do this work. I'll never be able to do it. But now it's like I opened up another path. It's for me to succeed."

Aileen then probes further into how such changes came about. "What I need to understand is that you were on one path, and the messages you were giving yourself were, 'Can't do this, I'm gonna fail, school sucks, what's the point of trying, the teachers are out to get me.' All that stuff. Can you remember when you started to change that—was there something that happened?"

Maria remembers a conversation with her grandmother that was significant in finding the new path. "Oh yeah, that's right . . . at the start of this year, all my cousins started getting pregnant, and that's when my grandmother came up to me and said, 'Ah well, babe, what do you want to do with your life?' And that's when I thought, 'Oh well, I can't be anything. I haven't got anything for myself.' She just pointed out to me life is what I make it. So if I want to be bad it's my fault. Why don't I succeed? And then she told me that in her day she didn't have any choice. All she was allowed to do was to get married and have babies, stay home and look after them. And then she pointed out to me that there's women out there, they're lawyers, they're anything they want to and your cousins are just getting pregnant and staying in the same place. And she goes, 'You're the only one left.' Just knowing that she believed in me made me believe in myself."

All this has been predicated on the externalizing of truancy with which Aileen and Maria began. It enabled Maria to avoid thinking of herself as a wagger by nature and to see truancy as a problem that existed in a set of social relations. The new path is also connected to important relationships in Maria's life. For a young Maori woman, a grandmother's advice has much salience, and the responses of teachers and friends constitute important shifts in reputation, which Maria now has to take into account as she thinks about who she is.

Enrolling a New Student

Sometimes, trouble has its way with young people to the extent that they do end up being asked to leave a particular school. When they arrive at the doors of a new school, they may end up speaking with the school counselor as part of the enrolment process. Rather than treating this interview as simply a formality, the counselor may construct it as an opportunity to develop a narrative conversation about trouble and its influence. The aim of this conversation might be to set up the enrolment at the new school as a turning point for a new experience of school. Reputations can follow a person from one school to another. The young person can bring with him or her a "troubled" identity. Therefore, the old story can simply be reproduced in a new context, fueling the idea that trouble originates in the essential core of such a person. The challenge is to establish a way of talking in which the effects of trouble do not completely subjugate the person's desire to live free of trouble.

Here are some questions that might be used to stimulate such a conversation:

- Do you want trouble to follow you here, or would you rather leave it at your other school?
- How might trouble try to trick you into letting it follow you?
- What would it mean to you to create a trouble-free life at this school?
- What do you know about how to achieve this?
- Who might be able to help you in your endeavor to create this kind of school career?
- Did trouble offer any excitements that you might miss if they were not around?
- Would anyone feel betrayed if you were to shut trouble out of your life?

Counseling and Discipline

Throughout this chapter, we have been talking about counseling in what might be called a "disciplinary" sense. This is different from much school counseling, which concentrates on family or educational issues. Sometimes, counselors have shied away from working with the kinds of issues that get young people in trouble with school authorities, preferring to leave that kind of work to others. Often counselors are concerned that this kind of work will get them too closely allied with school discipline processes and interfere with their freedom to provide supportive counseling for young people. It might also interfere with their role as advocates on behalf of young people to the school administration.

We think there is a useful role for counselors to play in these discipline issues, and we believe that a narrative perspective makes it clearer. The kind of conversation we have been talking about emphasizes the avoidance of the language of blame and shame.

When totalizing descriptions are bandied about, narrative counselors are primed to look for other possible stories about the person. Through the use of externalizing conversations, a school counselor can explore the meaning world in which the problem exists, including the language in which it is being described. This kind of conversation also opens space for the encouragement of responsibility and accountability at the same time as engaging in a deconstruction of the power relations operating in the school.

There is a sense, too, that all counseling conversations are disciplinary in nature. This is not discipline in a repressive mode, designed to correct and suppress wayward behavior, usually by means of punishment. It is discipline in a formative mode, using sophisticated techniques for shaping the character and behavior of young people. This is discipline in a positive sense. Children are taught to stand in line, wait their turn, identify with their age group and its predilections and desires, think of the world in the way that textbook knowledge would have them think, submit to examinations and grading systems, and define themselves and their chances in life in relation to these instruments. The school report card is as much a part of the disciplinary function of schools as the detention room.

Yet despite the evolving sophistication of the technology of schooling, the disciplinary power of the education system is never completely effective. People do not always completely fit the mold. In fact, there are many young people who live on the margins. They are not granted access to the privileges of the modern world. They sense they will not become the kind of people the school is shaping.

Repressive school discipline is usually about correcting the individual who is showing signs of rebellion. It can become a process of adjusting the person to the dominant discourse of the school. Counseling bent to this purpose can easily become repressive in nature. However, it does not have to be so. A narrative perspective allows a different focus. It is about exploring and renegotiating a young person's relationship with trouble in a way that allows for the young person's preferences to be expressed, but without falling into the trap of excusing abusive behavior.

5

Working in a Narrative Way With Groups, Classes, and Even Communities

BEYOND AN EXCLUSIVE FOCUS ON THE INDIVIDUAL

So far in this book, we have been speaking mainly about counselors working with individuals and their problems. However, the narrative perspective does not view the individual as the exclusive focus of counseling. The reason for this is that none of us is the sole author of any of the stories or discourses out of which our lives are produced. Our individual stories are at best threads woven into the social fabric of stories. The problems that we encounter in our lives develop in interactions that take place in communities. If we work to create changes in such interactions, we can effect changes in individual experience as well as changes in the climate of whole communities.

Narrative therapy grew out of a family therapy tradition that emphasized the role of the family as an "interpretive community" (Pare, 1995), but the focus on the nuclear family as the primary therapeutic unit can also be unnecessarily rigid and narrow. Schools, neighborhoods, friendship groups, social clubs, and sports teams are also communities in which discourses are continually evolving and changing. In order for the new stories that are produced in counseling to remain vibrant and develop in significance, they need to take root in the discourse of the school (or some other) community, not just in the minds of the client and the counselor.

This perspective leads the school counselor to start to think beyond the internal world of the individual who makes his way to the counselor's office. Once we have started to develop an alternative story with a client, we want to widen the focus quickly. We want the story to become known. A story isn't a story unless it finds an appreciative audience. The function of an audience is to hear the story as it is produced and to respond to it. Responses might include expressing appreciation or applauding, they might involve reviewing or publicizing the new story, or they might involve contributing to the development and evolution of the new story.

A counselor working in a narrative mode deliberately works with whatever community might be available to serve as the appreciative audience to the new story. This may mean drawing on the support of family members, it may mean setting up conferences with teachers, or it may mean recruiting other children into the appreciative elaboration of a new story. Caretakers, office staff, teacher aides, and sports coaches around the school community should also be remembered as potential audiences to a new story, as well as teachers, parents, and peers. These members of the school community may know important things about a young person and may contribute to the elaboration of what begins in counseling.

Family therapists have long advocated systemic interventions into the structure and communication of the family. Intervening in the structure and communication patterns of the school community is a parallel task for school counselors, but a school is much more complex than a family. Such complexity can be daunting for a counselor. The thought of trying to change the school in order to help each child can sound like an exhausting proposition. However, the complexity of the school community can be thought of as an advantage as well as a disadvantage. Complexity means diversity. It makes more likely the existence somewhere in the school of a "community of acknowledgement" (White, 1996) for each person's struggle. The more diverse the interpretive community, the more likely that someone will appreciate and support what a person is trying to become. The counselor's job becomes one of finding and fostering the interpretive connections.

This task does not have to involve working to produce large-scale structural changes to a school. That kind of project is not necessarily the counselor's role. Counselors are, however, trained in the art of conversation. They can play a role in shaping the kinds of conversations that take place in the school. This is where the concept of discourse is particularly useful. Discourse can be thought of as circulating through, and finding expression in, many conversations, ultimately shaping the thinking of people who participate in these conversations. Eventually, this thinking finds expression in the decisions that shape the organization of the school community. If we can make challenges that are transformative enough to dominant discourses, the effects of counseling can be felt in the structuring of life in the school. For counselors, working to change the discourse around specific problem issues is perhaps more manageable than operating directly on organizational structures and systems.

In this task, the school counselor has the advantage of easy and ready access to the school community. School counselors live in the midst of the discourse of the school in a way that family therapists do not live with the families who consult them. Moreover, because the school counselor's clients continue to be part of a school community after they have stopped wanting counseling, opportunities for follow-up on work done in counseling are manifold. Follow-up may include quick exchanges in the corridor or in the teachers' lounge as much as full counseling sessions.

When a stone is dropped into a pond, there is an initial splash followed by a series of concentric ripples that travel outward in all directions at once. This image is useful for explaining the concerns of narrative counselors (White, 1986). The counseling session may provide an initial splash, but the job of the counselor is to see that the ripples of a new story continue to flow outward and spread as far as possible. Ripples last longer than splashes, and they are not restricted to a local area of the pond. They can sometimes set the whole pond awash with a new story. What follows in this chapter are collected ideas for setting the school pond awash by encouraging the ripple effect. These ideas extend the impact of narrative counseling beyond what can be achieved in a one-to-one counseling interview.

Seeking out a Wider Audience to the New Story

Let us start with what can happen in an individual counseling session when the counselor maintains a wider focus. If we think of problems as originating in the discourse that is exchanged in conversations, then it makes sense to think of solutions to problems in the same way. The person we see in counseling is not just an individual struggling with her own thoughts and feelings, but is also a participant in a range of conversations and a variety of relationships. The process of re-authoring identities requires us to take account of the social nature of identity formation. The new identity needs to be recognized, appreciated, and elaborated. All these things involve other people. Therefore, when a fledgling new story is emerging in a counseling interview, we are very interested in who can play a part in its dissemination. The first step is to engage clients in identifying the people who might assist in promoting their identity projects. Here are some questions that might be asked to assist this process.

- ▨ Who else around the school would be the least surprised to hear you described as reliable/hardworking/trustworthy?
- ▨ Which of your teachers would be the first to notice your efforts to make these changes?
- ▨ Do you have any friends who would support you in a struggle against trouble?
- ▨ Has anyone noticed what you have achieved?

▓ What might this development mean to how other people in the school think of you?

Each of these questions brings another character into the story who might be prepared to join in the task of appreciative elaboration. Once this person is identified, the counselor and the client can work together to build in this person's involvement with the new story. Several options open up for the counselor working to elaborate the plot. They all involve moving the story out of the realm of internal dialogue and into the realm of interaction between people, that is, into the world of discourse. Each of the following strategies aims to prolong the ripple effect of a little splash outward into the school community.

▓ Have the student speculate about an imaginary conversation with this other person about the new story.

▓ Rehearse a plan for an actual future conversation aimed at acquainting this person more fully with new plot developments.

▓ Recall recent conversations with this person, and speculate further about the meanings of what he said.

▓ Invite the person into a counseling meeting in order to ask specifically for her contribution to the new story.

▓ Send this person a written report of the counseling meeting, including a mention of his name in relation to the recent plot developments.

▓ Invite this person to report back before the next counseling meeting on any further developments in the counterplot.

▓ Publish a document of acknowledgment for an achievement and circulate it among a young person's teachers.

▓ Ask permission of the child to go and speak directly with this person and prepare her for impending changes.

Counselors who are committed to ethical practice may wonder about such activities in terms of possible breaches of confidentiality.

Rest assured that narrative counseling does not mean abandoning ethical standards. None of this broadening of the focus of counseling should take place without the informed consent of the client. The dangers of circulating such stories around a community are also reduced by the narrative emphasis on stories of achievement rather than on stories of deficits or problems. In fact, in order to be an appreciative audience, it is usually not necessary for anyone even to know about the nature of the problem story. Few clients are concerned about their talents and abilities being publicized.

Building Communities of Concern

It has often been assumed in counseling that clients might not be interested in the common struggles in which other clients are engaged. This assumption privileges the counselor as the person who becomes the repository of experience and knowledge of how to combat problems. The sharing of such accumulated knowledge by the counselor bolsters the appearance of expertise by the counselor at the expense of opportunities for capitalizing on clients' knowledge. Clients can be invited to share their knowledge with each other. This has to be done within the bounds of confidentiality and with proper regard to informed consent. It can, however, lead to the establishment of little *communities of concern* in which people support each other to overcome a problem.

David Epston and others have been keen on establishing communities of concern among young women who have suffered at the hands of anorexia (Epston, Morris, & Maisel, 1995). The "anti-anorexia and bulimia" leagues have included young women who have been willing to share their experiences of the struggle to take back their lives from the grip of eating problems. They have forged a group solidarity in opposition to the dominant discourses of body image that have contributed to their problems with eating.

Associated with the establishment of a community of concern, usually among people combating a particular problem, is the building up of an "archive" of stories of successful attempts to undermine the problem. These can serve as a source of inspiration to others struggling with the same problem. They can be written by counselors and clients together and offered to new clients as tried and tested, useful ideas for breaking free of a problematic discourse. Or they might be made into videos in which the counselor interviews clients about how they have managed to claim their lives back from ano-rexia's or bulimia's iron grip.

The development of a community of concern also serves another purpose. It opens the way for changes in the relative positions of client and counselor. As the client starts to develop expertise in how to manage or defeat a particular problem, the counselor's task, from a narrative point of view, becomes one of consulting him carefully about the knowledge from which he is drawing. In other words, the counselor seeks to learn from the client and, in so doing, to lend her professional weight to the validation of the client's knowledge. One of the aims of this inquiry is to elaborate the story in which the client is an agent of change. Another aim is to reconstruct the politics of the counseling relationship in a way that grants significant privilege to the client's perspective.

In the political arrangement this kind of inquiry seeks to establish, the client is the expert. The counselor is seeking to consult her about what she knows. This consultation can be driven by simple curiosity or it can be specifically focused on collecting useful information to share with other clients. Either way, the counselor's role becomes one of scribe or recorder, rather than pronouncer of truths. To some extent, the usual politics of relations between professionals and their clients is subverted.

Here are some examples of problem issues around which commu-nities of concern have been established in some schools:

- the anti-anorexia and bulimia league
- the fear-busters and monster-tamers club
- the antisuspension league
- the antiharassment team
- the combating truancy list

The Antiharassment Team

Some especially creative work done in one school by two school counselors deserves highlighting. Aileen Cheshire and Dorothea Lewis (1996b), working at Selwyn College in Auckland, New Zealand, have achieved a significant impact in the life of their school with the establishment of a student-driven Antiharassment Team. It is a good example of counselors taking a wider view of their role and addressing the problems that were present in the discourse of the school rather than simply working with individuals to mitigate the effects of this discourse.

The concern that this project addressed was the prevalence of violent, bullying, or harassing behavior among young people. Selwyn College took a strong stand against violence in the school and set about the deliberate creation of a violence-free atmosphere. At the same time, the school was being required by legislative edict to develop a policy for dealing with sexual harassment. The Antiharassment Team was set up to address all forms of verbal, physical, and sexual harassment through a peer mediation service and consciousness-raising activities in the school. The team was carefully trained, and members took on a mediation role in a range of school disputes. The work of this team was so effective that belonging to the team became a sought-after position in the school, and the project won a national award for its work.

Dorothea and Aileen were both clearly informed by a narrative focus in establishing this team. It was an opportunity for them to share the mantle of expert with an enthusiastic group of young people who had much knowledge and resourcefulness to offer in the handling of local conflict situations. Their role became one of training and supporting the expression of student desires for a violence-free atmosphere. The same spirit was picked up by the student mediators, who worked to empower other students in challenging the influence of harassment or violence in the school. As the team's name suggests, the focus of the work is on combating the problem of harassment, not in blaming or shaming individual people. This is an embodiment of the narrative motto, "The problem is the problem, the person is not the problem." Mediation opens up space for the performance of alternative stories in conflict situations, and qualitatively different relationships can result. The aim of the team has always been an ambitious one: that of changing the culture of the school. Success in shifting the culture of the school is attested to by this sort of comment from one of the team members:

> I used to think, before I came to this school, that being hassled was just part of life, and you had to put up with it. Now I know differently.

Group Work Programs

The narrative emphasis on developing an appreciative audience for new developments in a person's life lends itself to group work. Groups provide a ready-made community of concern and many opportunities for the kind of interaction that opens possibilities for new ways of living. New identities can be rehearsed and tried out in the safe environment of a group before being taken out into a wider world. The isolating effects of a problem can be broken down by the very nature of group interaction.

Moreover, the life of a group itself can be spoken about in narrative terms. Any group develops its own story, the plot of which can be named and explored. Preferences for plot development can be intentionally created. Characters called forth by any particular plot or theme can be described, and group members can choose whether or not to enter into such characterizations.

The group can also be asked about problematic subplots that develop within the group's life, and these can be externalized so that no group member feels to blame for their effects. For example, the effects of secrecy, or conflict, or absence from the group can be inquired into. The effects of pervasive social discourses about gender, race, or class on the life of the group can be deconstructed. Individual experiences of such named problems can be explored, and a summary of the overall effects on the life of the whole group can be documented.

The Journey

An exciting illustration of the power of a narrative approach applied to group work has been provided by Aileen Cheshire and Dorothea Lewis in their innovative development of "The Journey" (Cheshire & Lewis, 1996a). The Journey is a group project that students who want to experience themselves in new ways volunteer to enter. It is an adventure-based program that takes place in an outdoor education setting. What distinguishes it from many other outdoor programs is its deliberate emphasis on the re-authoring of young people's stories about themselves.

A feature of the program is the careful preparation that goes into each person's participation in the group. The program is widely advertised in the school for anyone between 15 and 18 years. It is promoted to those students who have already begun to make substantial changes in their lives and also to those who urgently want to turn their lives around. Applicants are asked to answer the following narrative-informed questions:

■ Please tell us about what attracts you to apply for The Journey?
■ What qualities do you have that might help you succeed?
■ Which of these qualities would you like to develop more?
■ What would you like to be different when The Journey is finished?

This entry point invites the students right from the outset to begin to develop alternative stories about themselves that emphasize their strengths, competencies, and abilities. Thus, the therapeutic work is already under way well before the students begin the program.

Students are then interviewed in a style that builds upon the written application. For some, The Journey is the last opportunity to make changes before being suspended from school.

Andrew was one such person. He told Aileen, "Something has to change. I've got to do something, because nothing's worked so far. Things are pretty bad."

Aileen and Dorothea ask questions of people like Andrew, such as, "What is it about The Journey that has led you to hope that this could be a way of having a different future?" "Do you have ideas about the things in yourself that you would like to feel better about?"

They listened carefully to what Andrew had to say about the changes he would like to make and the different kind of future he envisaged. They expressed curiosity about what The Journey meant to him, both now and for his future.

Where possible, families are included as the participants prepare for The Journey. Family members can help create an environment where personal changes are encouraged and supported. Aileen met with Andrew's aunt and asked her whether the goals Andrew had set himself were what she would have expected or whether there were some surprises.

She responded, "I'm absolutely blown away by what he wants to do. I think these are wonderful."

The successful applicants first of all participate in 2 days of adventure-based learning, negotiating their way along ropes on a confidence course. In the process, they develop commitments to each other and to the group process. Then there are three group meetings at school that focus on preparing the group for The Journey itself. Finally, the students are ready for the 300-mile journey, which takes them 10 days of hiking, cycling, and sea kayaking.

In the group sessions, before departing for The Journey, the group watches a video of their first adventure-based experience. This provides opportunities to notice changes that are already taking place in the participants' lives and in the group life. Dorothea and Aileen express curiosity about what the young people see on the video. They encourage the making of meaning around developmental steps that the group is taking together. Here are some of the questions that are asked:

- What do you notice about the way the group is working?
- Is there anything you notice about yourself at the end of the 2 days that is different from how you were at the beginning?

The responses given are often in stark contrast to the experiences these young people have of themselves prior to entry into this program.

Prior to departure on The Journey, the group also explores the challenges that they are facing to their preparation. For example, many face invitations from friends to be sidetracked into older, troublesome habits. Living an "On the Edge Lifestyle" might be storied at this point as an obstacle to what they want to achieve on The Journey. The group members explore how they can support each other to break through such obstacles.

Then, The Journey itself begins. Each day has a different student leader. The day is introduced with a story or a reading emphasizing themes that run through the entire day, such as "a temporary community," "new beginnings," "risks," and "perseverance." Halfway through The Journey, counselors have individual sessions with the group members. Prior to these sessions, individuals are primed to notice developments in themselves during the adventure. This interview continues the development of the preferred story. Aileen and Dorothea's purpose is to develop a coherent account of what students have been experiencing, thinking, and feeling. The following kinds of questions facilitate this kind of storybuilding:

- Have there been things that you have done that at first you didn't think you could do?
- What was it that enabled you to do that?
- Now you know this about yourself, what difference does it make?

These questions are carefully sculptured to bring forth the maximum amount of personal reflection and review of these young peoples' lives.

They also ask audience questions to give these adventurers a chance to review their lives from the perspective of significant others, such as:

- Who would be least surprised at you doing that?
- What do you think that person would say to you now?

By the time the group returns home, the careful preparation and constant reflection on preferred directions has often produced life-changing results. For example, Rachel reported when she returned, "This is the very first time I haven't given up on myself. I am helping myself for the very first time. I've always given up on myself before and I know that, although I felt like giving up, this time I didn't!"

The follow-up to The Journey is also important to its ongoing effectiveness. Participants have to reenter regular school life. Without support, there is the danger that the strength of the new stories can quickly fade in the face of peer stresses that reassert their influence. While students are very busy catching up with school activities, they also participate in further group meetings, individual counseling, family meetings, and a final 2-day group experience, all aimed at consolidating and publicizing the new identities developed during The Journey. A photographic montage is given to each student, certificates are presented, and therapeutic letters written to each participant.

Aileen and Dorothea report that the real success of The Journey is reflected in the comments of students who completed the program in previous years. They report that it has been after a substantial period of time that students realized the true impact of The Journey on their lives. The hope is that in the future, these students can always utilize these powerful experiences to make new meanings on their life journey.

Working With a Whole Class

Often, a whole class gets a reputation in a school community that builds up around a particular problem. For example, a class can get a reputation for being noisy, argumentative, poorly behaved, or always late arriving. Sometimes, too, a particular problem can take root in the culture of a particular class without being associated with any specific individual. A culture of teasing putdowns or bullying and intimidation are examples of such problems. They can make life unhappy for many members of a class. Conflicts can also develop between groups in a class and then start to structure the mood of the whole class.

In these situations, individual counseling is not the most effective approach to building an alternative story. It is quicker to work with the whole class. The same principles of narrative thinking apply. The problem is explored and named in an externalizing, nonblaming way. The problem is blamed for the unhappiness in the class rather than the class members. The problem story is treated as a partial truth rather than a complete picture of the life of the class, and totalizing descriptions of the class are contested by uncovering alternative aspects of the life of the class. Then the class is invited to re-story its own reputation as it would prefer to be known, and teachers are issued invitations to notice this class identity as it grows. Let us tell the story of a particularly creative piece of work with a class.

A Case Study

Pamela Gray-Yeates (1997), a school psychologist, introduced a narrative antibullying program into a local elementary school. She began with a class whose teacher was particularly interested in addressing bullying and violence. If this was well received, she planned to extend the project to include the school and the community. She worked with 7- and 8-year-olds over a period of 5 weeks, meeting with the class twice a week.

Pamela began by brainstorming with the class a list of the things that stood in the way of children getting along with each other. She documented their ideas and checked with the children on the accuracy of the summary, which she presented in the following session. Already, she was conveying to the children that their views were important and that she would take them seriously.

Through this inquiry, bullying was identified by the children as a problem in the class. All the children recognized that they had, on occasion, been bullies, victims, or passive observers to bullying acts. The recognition that all the children had been involved in bullying behavior encouraged them to move away from simply dividing up the class into separate camps of bullies and victims.

Next, Pamela historicized bullying by asking the children where they had learned so much about it. "Where is bullying and teasing most likely to happen?" she asked. The children told their own stories about being victims of bullying and drew pictures of the effects of bullying on themselves and their classmates.

Pamela asked about what might get in the way of children who wanted to give up bullying. This question helped the children recognize the power of the problem and the difficulty of challenging the regime of bullying. She gave them an exercise in which they decided on a 1-to-10 scale how strong their desire was to eradicate bullying.

This exercise was repeated on a further two occasions to monitor the children's commitment toward creating a nonviolent class.

The children were asked to imagine what it would be like to have bullying walk out of the school and disappear over the horizon. She led a visualization exercise where the children imagined what it might be like for teachers, parents, and young people in a peaceful environment. The children made a collage of this visualization. The contrast between a dominant problem story and a desirable alternative one was growing.

Then the children took part in a puppet show. Pamela had developed a script from the children's earlier stories of being violated. A bully monster appeared with a mop of white wiry hair, green eyes, and a spiky tail. Its primary intention was to humiliate, taunt, and demonstrate aggression. The content was compelling for the children, because the bully monster was enacting their own scenarios. Some were confronted with their own behavior. The bully monster had other friends, such as Lex the Liar and Tooch. Lex was a weaselly creature who wore a pink cape and had long curly antennae protruding out of its beak-like head. Tooch looked like a fly with big eyes, webbed wings, and a long black tongue. His job was to pick on anyone feeling beaten down by the bully monster. He would taunt and abuse those who were already feeling victimized. The children wrote scripts illustrating the favorite tactics of this gang of three.

There were three other puppets. One of them was Buffum, a child puppet of no specific gender. It had brown skin and long scruffy hair. This puppet represented the peaceful children in the school. Buffum also had two friends. Freelum was a friendly witch who could put spells on bullying monsters. The children developed the script for Freelum's magic spell.

Giddle de doo, rumplety dum, look in the mirror and see yourself run.
Breathe in your poison, cough up your fear,
Taste your own meanness and shrivel up here!

The other friend of Freelum and Buffum was Lovealot, who was peaceful, kind, and loving, even to the despicable Tooch. He used this ability to disarm the bully and his sneaky friends.

The children then enacted stories in which the bully monster was defeated by its own wickedness. One story line had the bully monster so isolated from its friends that it was embraced by Buffum and invited to join some new friends who had fun without bullying. As they developed these stories, Pamela asked the children to draw from their own experience of peaceful, respectful interactions that stood in contrast with hurtful, abusive ones. Their scripts matched anything that could have been produced by a social skills training program. They literally put their indigenous knowledge on show.

Pamela read the class a story that featured the children's ideas on combating bullying. Then she asked the children about times when they were nearly involved in a bullying act but ended up taking a stand against bullying. These stories were gathered together in a new, nonviolent, classwide identity. Each child had an opportunity to describe an event where he or she made the bully monster smaller. Then the children constructed a large mural showing some of the tricks they had discovered to defeat the bully monster. The puppet shows continued with even more sophisticated interactions with the bully monster and its friends. The children began to become experts on peer abuse and made pamphlets to inform other children of what they had learned. Some became class activists against peer abuse.

Then the children made a video about the class's expertise in making bullying smaller. Their knowledge was also used to make antibullying posters to display around the school. They wrote letters to parents explaining the class stand against bullying.

By now, the class teacher was noticing significant changes in the children's behavior. They had an immediate awareness of when bullying entered the class and could name it as such. They no longer blamed themselves if they were victims of bullying. Previously, many children would have remained quiet about peer abuse because they had thought it was something that happened only to them. Small outbreaks of bullying still go on from time to time, but the teacher felt that the program had been enormously effective. Some parents responded to the value of the program. One parent noted that her child had been bullied over a long period of time because of her ethnicity. She called to say that her daughter no longer felt responsible for the bullying and would tell someone if it happened again.

Over the next few weeks, the teacher continued to ask the children about steps they had taken to get the better of bullying. She and Pamela were amazed at the knowledge that the children presented. They had not been positioned as passive recipients but as experts, and they had responded with enthusiasm.

Pamela is planning to develop this program on a school- and communitywide basis to involve other school staff and parents.

Classroom Lessons Built on "Interviewing the Problem"

Often, school counselors are asked to teach lessons on health or psychoeducational topics. The narrative technique of externalizing the problem lends itself admirably to discussions of sensitive or controversial topics in such lessons. For example, a health education lesson on drugs and alcohol can be built around a personification of the problem. The sociodramatic technique of "interviewing the problem" (Roth & Epston, 1996) can be employed. Here is a step-by-step plan for a lesson based on this approach.

1. Introduce the topic and tell the class that they are very privileged to be granted a rare interview with "Drugs" today and so, "This is a chance to ask about many things that you might have wondered." Explain that the aim of the exercise is to explore the relationship between the problem and people like the class members, but to do so from the problem's perspective rather than from the human perspective.

2. Invite two or three volunteers to play the role of Drugs. Instruct them that they are not to think of themselves as people at all. They are actually Drugs. Tell them to spend a few minutes preparing themselves to be Drugs by thinking about some things they might want to get across in the interview. The exercise will work with a single volunteer playing the role of the problem, but with three people sharing the role, there is a chance to demonstrate the complexities of a problem because each of the characterizations of Drugs can

be a little different. For example, one of the team playing Drugs may focus everyone's attention on the "good time" excitement that drugs offer people. Another might play the role of persuading the audience that drugs will make them feel better in the face of problems. These different roles may be imagined by each of the three people thinking of some situation they have come across or heard about in which drugs have had an influence in someone's life. The role of Drugs can be concretized by developing a particular scenario in which Drugs play a part with a cast of characters who can be named. This scenario should be one that is relevant to the lives of the class members.

3. Instruct the rest of the class to take on the role of news reporters who are gathering for a press conference being granted by Drugs. Their job is to think up some questions to ask Drugs. They can take a few minutes to prepare these questions. Their task is to ask the kind of questions that will enable them to learn about people's drug problems from Drugs's perspective.

4. Box 5.1 lists topics the reporters can ask about. This list can be given to the reporters on a piece of paper.

5. Conduct the interview (about 15 minutes), and ask the class to take careful notes about what Drugs says.

6. After the interview has uncovered sufficient material about the tactics Drugs uses to influence young people, interrupt the interview and suggest a change of topic. This time, the reporters should ask Drugs questions aimed at exposing its failures and worries. How have young people been able to resist its influence and made it feel demoralized? This is investigative journalism, so encourage the reporters to ask the really tough questions, the ones that will make Drugs squirm with discomfort and embarrassment. In effect, an alternative story of resistance to Drugs's influence is opened up here (see Box 5.2).

7. When the second part of the interview is completed, all class members become themselves again. Take care to de-role properly the people who have been playing Drugs. De-roling can be done by asking them to stand up and move seats and, as they move, to leave

---

BOX 5.1

Problem Exploration Topics to Ask "Drugs" About

■ Its purposes in life

■ Its hopes and dreams for young people's lives

■ The techniques it uses to get young people on its side

■ The tricks or methods of persuasion it uses to get its own way

■ What it likes to hear young people saying or doing

■ With whom or what it makes friends and works in league with

■ What makes its work especially easy or difficult

Sample Questions

■ Drugs, what are some of your favorite methods of getting into someone's life? Are there some circumstances in which you find it easier to persuade young people to join your team? What are they?

■ What do you promise young people when they are a bit reluctant to listen to you?

■ If people do start to do what you are telling them to do, what sort of life do you plan out for them?

■ What do you try to convince a person of about himself or herself in order to make him or her more susceptible to your persuasion?

■ Do you have different tactics with girls and boys?

Drugs on the chair on which they were sitting. When they have moved, ask them to say out loud to the class three ways in which they are different from the role they have been playing.

8. The final stage of the lesson is to discuss what came out of the interview and to reflect on it. Box 5.3 suggests some questions to stimulate this discussion.

BOX 5.2

Re-Storying Questions Topics to Ask "Drugs" About

▪ Methods young people have used to frustrate Drugs's plans and best efforts to take control of their lives

▪ Occasions Drugs has noticed young people resisting its influence

▪ Threats to its power to influence young people

▪ Plans Drugs might have to reassert itself against such threats

Sample Questions

▪ What are some of the things you don't like to hear young people saying?

▪ What really upsets you or demoralizes you?

▪ Give us some examples of your most embarrassing failures.

▪ What can young people do that almost makes you give up?

This exercise can be a lot of fun. It can also generate some unusual ways of talking about a problem issue that make way for changes to taken-for-granted ways of thinking. Of course, a range of other issues can be substituted for Drugs in this example.

Starting Conversations With a School

A narrative counselor needs to be alert to the aspects of the school community that make it unique. She needs to listen carefully to the language of the school, to develop an ear for discourse, particularly for the dominant stories that are constitutive of life in that community, some of them common to many school contexts, some of them peculiar to the local school.

In some senses, the whole school can be thought of as the counselor's client. She can listen to the school speak. This means listening to the effects of dominant stories on the people in the school—pupils,

---

BOX 5.3

Reflection Questions

▨ What was it like to be Drugs? To be a reporter?

▨ What did you find surprising or interesting in this interview?

▨ How was this conversation about drugs different from other discussions about this problem?

▨ What might you take from this interview that might be useful in the future?

---

teachers, parents, and nonteaching staff. There will be much that is nonproblematic about how relations and identities are constituted within such discourse, but from time to time, a counselor will hear stories of recurrent unhappiness or frustration or injustice.

Not all of these issues are best addressed by working with individuals in counseling. The counselor can play a significant role as change agent in the school. This idea, however, begs the question, "How do you engage a whole school in conversation?" The skills of advocacy and consultation, rather than clinical counseling, are relevant here. The same narrative concepts can guide this professional task: listening to problem stories, mapping their effects, seeking out unique outcomes, and fostering the development of a counterplot.

One high school counselor, who was concerned about expressions of racism in a school, collaborated with the school drama teacher, who shared a concern to do something about this issue. Together, they asked a senior drama class to develop some enactments of typical instances that illustrated this problem and its effects on people. They used the dramatic technique of "interviewing the problem" as described above. Several members of the drama class took on the personified voice of "Racism." Then the rest of the class interviewed Racism about its tactics and desires and hopes for the young people in the school. In this way, they opened for view the discourses in which racism operated, but in a way that did not place blame on anyone. An externalizing conversation was conducted in a highly dramatic way.

They also inquired into occasions when racism was not allowed to hold sway, or when the young people in the school took a stand against racism. The result was a witty and humorous drama in which the ideas about combating the influence of Racism emerged completely from the young people's knowledge. This drama was then performed in front of school assemblies. Afterward, the school counselor visited classes and talked to them about their ideas for furthering the counterplot to the story of Racism.

This is an example of proactive work by a school counselor, thinking outside of the square of the prototypical counseling interview, but it was just as surely aimed at improving young people's experience of school as any individual counseling session. There are many other ways in which this can be done.

Another approach was taken by Lynn, a school counselor who had become concerned about the rate of suspensions of Maori children from her school. She suspected that there would be concern about these matters in the Maori community, but she was not hearing it expressed in the school. Her response to this situation was to ask if she could attend the local meetings of the Maori Women's Welfare League (a nationally organized voluntary welfare organization). She was made welcome at these meetings, although there was some suspicion about her purposes at first. Was she there as a representative of the school, spying on the Maori community? She reassured them that her intention was quite different. She was interested in listening to the concerns of the community about what was happening in the school and in helping to get these concerns heard in the school. She became instrumental in asking the school to address some of these concerns and, in this way, addressing some of the influences of institutional racism on school suspensions.

Another way to work with a whole school is to think about the narrative effects of the systems of communication and documentation that are used in a school. Do they facilitate only the telling of problem stories about young people, or do they open possibilities for schools to appreciate alternative stories? Do they encourage totalizing descriptions of people, or do they leave room for appreciating the contradictory aspects of a person? Do they locate problems in the "nature" of individuals, or do they take account of the operation of power in the construction of personhood? Do they encourage professional accountability to the pupils and their parents in a school community, or do they promote a one-way view of accountability that bolsters the position of teachers, school administrators, and counselors at the expense of young people? Do they give opportunity for young people's voices to be heard, or do they privilege only the voices of adults?

The answers to such questions can lead a counselor to become involved in the redesigning of school procedures and documents so that they are compatible with a narrative philosophy. Such work can facilitate the reverberation of new stories around the school. It is therapeutic in an organizational sense.

Narrative Climate in the School

In the previous section, we considered what might happen if a school counselor took on board the vision of working with the stories that are on the loose in a school. We can only speculate about what might happen if a whole school developed a commitment to thinking in narrative terms. Let us end this book with some speculation about what this kind of school might begin to look like.

1. Students and their families, and, for that matter, teachers, would not be spoken about in ways that presumed to capture the essential truth about them in a totalizing form. Pupils would not be described as if laziness or disruptiveness was who they were. School documents would be circumspect and tentative in their descriptions of people because teachers would be aware of the power of their words to create people's lives, not just describe them. School reports would therefore be written as provisional accounts rather than definitive statements about the teacher's "knowledge" of the student's character. All descriptions would take care to avoid proscribing people's lives within a narrow band of possibility. Moreover, the primary focus of such descriptions would be upon appreciating talents and competencies, rather than on diagnosing deficits. An ethic would develop in the school requiring that no one was spoken about behind his or her back in ways that could not be said respectfully to his or her face.

2. The school would build into its functioning a consciousness of power relations and reflexive processes by which those in positions of privilege were constantly held accountable for their power. The voices of children would be taken seriously and their knowledge respected for the expertise it offered. Teachers would be genuinely interested in learning from children, rather than automatically assuming that they knew better.

3. The school would encourage conversations that were deconstructive of the dominant stories operating within the school. Minority voices of all kinds would be actively solicited and ensured legitimate status in the politics of the school.

4. Whenever a problem came to attention in the school, it would be thought of as a story, or as a construction of reality. Other possible constructions would be deliberately sought out. Unstoried experiences would be highly valued. Multiple and diverse perspectives would be thought of as enriching a community. Alternative stories would be investigated and mined for the hidden resources they might offer.

5. Narrative thinking would enter into even the curriculum and evaluation processes of the school. Knowledge would always be taught as a cultural product rather than as absolute reality. Postmodern questions about the dominance of a particular narrow range of rational thinking as the one way to establish truth would be opened up for young people to think about. Power relations as they are expressed in discourse would become subjects of study. Evaluation methods would not focus in a judgmental way so strenuously on the individual, but would serve purposes of appreciating and elaborating conversations and communities.

These may sound like idealistic dreams. A cynical view might dismiss them as unlikely. We can only retort with John Lennon, "You may say I'm a dreamer, but I'm not the only one."

Moreover, the narrative perspective allows us to take encouragement from noticing that all of these ideals are in fact already happening. They are not yet writ large, but they are there under our noses in some embryonic or incipient form, in some unique outcomes, in some unrecognized and underdeveloped shape. The act of looking for them and noticing them when they occur is what translates them from idealistic dreams to plot developments in a real story.

This is what makes a narrative approach powerful. The idea that stories or discourses create people's lives is a rather simple idea, but it has huge implications if we take it seriously. Assuming stories to be as powerful as realities opens the door to wide-ranging possibilities that are not available if we stick with what is real or "realistic." At the same time, narrative thinking is not to be confused with wild-eyed enthusiasm, disconnected from the exigencies and vicissitudes of life. The optimism and enthusiasm built into a narrative counseling method is tempered by, and even founded on, a rigorous analysis of the operation of power in people's lives. When we seek out and work to develop an alternative story, it is not a fanciful dream we are creating, but an elaboration of what is already known. The search for and close attention paid to the possibilities of what already exists ensures that narrative optimism remains attuned to what is actual and possible.

At the same time, we hope that the examples we have given in this book make it clear that the narrative approach we are advocating makes possible some quite sharp, even dramatic, shifts in perspective. These shifts can have significant consequences in people's lives. Their power lies in the fact that they can make a real difference.

Reading List

Here are some selected readings for you to follow up on your interest in the practice of narrative counseling. They are chosen with a view to the needs of busy practitioners and arranged in a rough order of suggested relevance to school counseling.

Monk, G., Winslade, J., Crocket, K., & Epston, D. (1997). *Narrative therapy in practice: The archaeology of hope.* San Francisco: Jossey-Bass.

Freeman, J., Epston, D., & Lobovits, D. (1997). *Playful approaches to serious problems: Narrative therapy with children and their families.* New York: Norton.

Freedman, J., & Combs, G. (1996). *Narrative therapy: The social construction of preferred reality.* New York: Norton.

Jenkins, A. (1990). *Invitations to responsibility: The therapeutic engagement of men who are violent and abusive.* Adelaide, Australia: Dulwich Centre Publications.

McLean, C. (Ed.). (1995). Schooling and education: Exploring new possibilities [Special edition]. *Dulwich Centre Newsletter,* No. 2 & 3.

Smith, C., & Nylund, D. (1997). *Narrative therapies with children and adolescents.* New York: Guilford.

White, M. (1989a). The externalizing of the problem and the re-authoring of lives and relationships. In *Selected papers*. Adelaide, Australia: Dulwich Centre Publications.

White, M. (1989b). The process of questioning: A therapy of literary merit? In *Selected papers*. Adelaide, Australia: Dulwich Centre Publications.

White, M. (1992). Deconstruction and therapy. In D. Epston & M. White (Eds.), *Experience, contradiction, narrative and imagination*. Adelaide, Australia: Dulwich Centre Publications.

White, M., & Epston, D. (1991). *Narrative means to therapeutic ends.* New York: Norton.

The journals that most regularly feature articles on narrative therapy are:

The Dulwich Centre Newsletter
The Journal of Systemic Therapies

A Narrative Glossary

Alternative story: The story that develops in counseling in contradiction to the dominant story in which the problem holds sway.

Coauthoring: The ideal therapeutic relation in which both counselor and client share responsibility for the development of alternative stories.

Counterplot: The significant events in the development of the alternative story.

Deconstruction: The process of unpacking the taken-for-granted assumptions and underlying ideas behind social practices that masquerade as truth or reality. It is achieved by bringing to light the gaps or inconsistencies in a text or discourse or dominant story so that it no longer appears inevitable to accept what has seemed impossible to be otherwise. It is less adversarial and more playful than critique or confrontation.

Deficit description: Diagnostic description of a person that implies that the person does not measure up to an established norm.

Discourse: A set of ideas that can be embodied as structuring statements that underlie and give meaning to social practices, personal experience, and organizations or institutions. They often include the taken-for-granted assumptions that allow us to know how to go on in social situations of all kinds. They are linguistic in nature (provided that language is taken to include nonverbal practices as well as verbal).

Dominant story: The "normal" way of understanding a situation or the set of assumptions about an issue that has become so ingrained or widely accepted within a culture that it appears to represent "reality."

Externalizing conversation: A way of speaking in which a gap is introduced between the person and the problem issue. The problem may be spoken of as if it is a distinct entity or even a personality in its own right rather than closely identified with the person. This way of speaking opens space for te relationship between the person and the problem to be articulated.

Gaze: Processes of evaluation and isolation of individuals or groups of persons that serve to subjugate them to authorities and invite them to monitor or discipline themselves as if they are constantly being watched.

Internalizing conversations: Ways of speaking that locate problem issues firmly in the personality of the person who is suffering under them.

Mapping-the-influence questions: Questions asked about an externalized problem to detail the relationship between the person and the problem. The map may be about the influence of the problem on the person or about the influence of the person on the problem.

Postmodernism: A philosophical movement across a variety of disciplines that has set about dismantling many of the assumptions that underlie the established truths of the modern era.

Re-authoring: The process of developing an alternative story in therapy. In narrative counseling, this is jointly undertaken by the counselor and the client.

Self-description: A term used in narrative conversations for the identities human beings adopt. It is a usage that points to the provisional nature of all identities and to the possibilities of other descriptions, rather than toward a fixed, essential personality.

Totalizing descriptions: Descriptions that reduce the complexity of a person to an all-embracing single description that purports to capture the enduring essence of the person.

Unique outcome: An aspect of lived experience that lies outside of, or in contradiction to, the problem story; an opening to an alternative story.

References

Bateson, G. (1972). *Steps to an ecology of mind.* New York: Ballantine.

Bateson, G. (1980). *Mind and nature: A necessary unity.* New York: Bantam.

Bruner, E. (1986). Ethnography as narrative. In V. Turner & E. Bruner (Eds.), *The anthropology of experience* (pp. 139-155). Chicago: University of Illinois Press.

Cheshire, A., & Lewis, D. (1996a). The journey: A narrative approach to adventure-based therapy. *Dulwich Centre Newsletter,* 4, 7-16.

Cheshire, A., & Lewis, D. (1996b). *Taking the hassle out of school: The work of the anti-harassment team at Selwyn College.* Auckland, New Zealand: Selwyn College.

Epston, D., Morris, F., & Maisel, R. (1995). A narrative approach to so-called anorexia/bulimia. In K. Weingarten (Ed.), *Cultural resistance: Challenging beliefs about men, women, and therapy* (pp. 69-96). New York: Haworth.

Foucault, M. (1973). *The birth of the clinic.* London: Tavistock.

Foucault, M. (1979). *The archaeology of knowledge.* London: Penguin.

Freeman, J., Epston, D., & Lobovits, D. (1997). *Playful approaches to serious problems: Narrative therapy with children and their families.* New York: Norton.

Gergen, K. J. (1985). The social constructionist movement in modern psychology. *American Psychologist, 40*(3), 266-275.

Gergen, K. J. (1990). Therapeutic professions and the diffusion of deficit. *The Journal of Mind and Behavior, 11*(3-4), 353-368.

Gergen, K. J. (1994). *Realities and relationships: Soundings in social constructionism.* Cambridge, MA: Harvard University Press.

Gray-Yeates, P. (1997). *Re-authoring classroom identities: A narrative approach to working with children in the prevention of peer abuse.* Unpublished M. Couns. dissertation, University of Waikato, Hamilton, New Zealand.

Hoffman, L. (1992). A reflexive stance for family therapy. In S. McNamee & K. Gergen (Eds.), *Therapy as social construction* (pp. 7-24). Thousand Oaks, CA: Sage.

Hoshmand, L. T., & Polkinghorne, D. (1992). Redefining the science-practice relationship and professional training. *American Psychologist, 47*(1), 55-66.

Jenkins, A. (1990). *Invitations to responsibility: The therapeutic engagement of men who are violent and abusive.* Adelaide, Australia: Dulwich Centre Publications.

Pare, D. (1995). Of families and other cultures: The shifting paradigm of family therapy. *Family Process, 34*, 1-19.

Roth, S., & Epston, D. (1996). Consulting the problem about the problematic relationship: An exercise for experiencing a relationship with an externalized problem. In M. Hoyt (Ed.), *Constructive therapies II.* New York: Guilford.

Stewart, B., & Nodrick, B. (1990). The learning disabled lifestyle: From reification to liberation. *Family Therapy Case Studies, 5*(1), 61-73.

White, M. (1986). Negative explanation, restraint and double description: A template for family therapy. *Family Process, 25*(2), 169-184.

White, M. (1989a). The externalizing of the problem and the re-authoring of lives and relationships. *Dulwich Centre Newsletter* [Special edition, Summer 1988-1989], pp. 3-21.

White, M. (1989b). The process of questioning: A therapy of literary merit? In *Selected papers* (pp. 37-46). Adelaide, Australia: Dulwich Centre Publications.

White, M. (1992). Deconstruction and therapy. In D. Epston & M. White (Eds.), *Experience, contradiction, narrative & imagination* (pp. 109-152). Adelaide, Australia: Dulwich Centre Publications.

White, M. (1995). *Re-authoring lives: Interviews and essays.* Adelaide, Australia: Dulwich Centre Publications.

White, M. (1996). Schools as communities of acknowledgement. *Dulwich Centre Newsletter,* (No. 2 & 3), pp. 57-59.

White, M., & Epston, D. (1992). *Narrative means to therapeutic ends.* New York: Norton.

Index

Abusive behavior, combating:
   apologies, 88-89
   engagement of people in the
      process of changing. *See*
      Invitations to responsibility
   externalize the restraints to
      respectful behavior, 82-84
   perpetrators of abusive
      behavior, 78
   recipients of abusive behavior, 77
   taking action, facilitate, 86-88
Adventure-based program, 104-107
Alternative stories, 11-13, 25, 44-47,
   122
   See also individual subject headings
Antiharassment team, 102-103
Apologies for past abusive actions,
   88-89
Appreciative audience to new
   developments, 15-16, 96
Assembling the alternative story,
   44-47
Assumptions in the narrative
   approach, starting, 21

alternative discourses, aligning
   with, 25
comparing one phenomenon
   with another, 27-28
cultural story, dominant, 26
deconstructing dominant
   discourses, 26
discourses, embedded within
   stories lie, 22-24
lived experience does not
   always get encapsulated in
   stories, 27
stories, human beings live their
   lives according to, 22
surveillance/scrutiny, modern
   world characterized by norms
   kept in place by, 24-25
vacuum, stories we live by are
   not produced in a, 22
Attention deficit with
   hyperactivity (ADHD), 61-62
Attitudes to bring into the room:
   coauthorship, 30-31
   curiosity and persistence, 29

knowledge, respect for the
client's, 29-30
optimism and respect, 28-29

Bateson, Gregory, 21, 27
Belief systems, 24
Breadth and the externalized
problem, 39
Bruner, Edward, 21, 27
Bruner, Jerome, 21

Caution about using narrative
methods, 49-50
Checklist to use in mapping the
effects of the externalized
problem, 39-41
Cheshire, Aileen, ix
Classroom, troublesome behavior
in the:
documenting progress, 76
groups/classes and
communities, working with,
107-111
principles and strategies for
narrative counselors, 72-73
questions to ask the client, 73
social control mechanisms
supported by counseling,
71-72
who-the-hell-are-you tone, 74-75
Classroom lessons built on
technique of interviewing the
problem, 111-114
Client-centered listening, 32, 68
Coauthorship, 30-31, 122
Communication patterns of school
community, 96, 116
See also Groups/classes and
communities, working with
Communities of concern, building,
100-103
See also Groups/classes and
communities, working with

Comparing one phenomenon with
another, 27-28
Competence and ability, client's
areas of, 6, 10-11, 13-15, 41-43
Complexity of the school
community, 97
Concentric pond ripples analogy,
97-98
Controversial topics, discussion of,
111-114
Conversations taking place in the
school, counselors shaping
the, 97
See also Groups/classes and
communities, working with;
Schooling, the discourse of
Counselors shaping conversations
taking place in the school, 97
See also Groups/classes and
communities, working with;
Schooling, the discourse of
Crocket, Kathie, ix
Cultural story, dominant. *See*
Discourses; Dominant story;
Schooling, the discourse of
Curiosity, respectful, 6-7, 13, 29, 87
Cyclical progression, thinking in
terms of, 49

Deconstructing dominant
discourses, 26, 44, 59, 122
Deficit discourse:
criminality, 69-70
defining, 122
externalizing conversations, 36
local knowledge, erosion of, 63-64
normality, describing, 59-60
professionals, reliance on, 62-63
resistance to deficit-based
descriptions, 64-66
self-enfeeblement, personal, 60-62
Depth and the externalized
problem, 40

Descriptions:
　medicalized, 61-62
　personifications, developing
　　externalizing descriptions
　　into, 38-39
　redescription process, 65-66
　resistance to deficit-based, 64-66
　school, 53-57
　self-description, 123
　totalizing, 5-6, 70, 116
Disciplinary sense, counseling in a,
　93-94
　See also Abusive behavior,
　　combaing
Discourses:
　alternative, aligning with, 25
　deconstructing dominant
　　discourses, 26
　defining, 122-123
　embedded within stories lie, 22-24
　reversing internalizing logic of
　　taken-for-granted, 38
　See also Deficit discourse;
　　Schooling, the discourse of
Documenting changes, 18-19,
　47-49, 76, 116-117
Dominant story:
　abusive behavior, 82
　attractiveness, 24-25
　deconstructing dominant
　　discourses, 26, 44, 59, 122
　defining, 123
　externalizing conversations, 36
　gender-based subject choices, 59
　limits created by, 26
　See also Discourses; Schooling,
　　the discourse of
Drewery, Wendy, ix
Drug use, 112-115

Eating problems, 24-25
End-of-term report on progress in
　problem busting, 48

Enrolling a new student, 92-93
Epston, David, vii, 21, 35
Ethical care to speak in respectful
　ways, 59
Externalizing conversations:
　abusive behavior, combating,
　　82-84
　checklist to use in mapping the
　　effects of the externalized
　　problem, 39-41
　competence, detecting clues to,
　　41-43
　defining, 123
　developing, suggestions for, 37-39
　examples, 36
　opens space to create a lighter
　　approach, 35
　parody of dominant cultural
　　stories, 36
　scenario, a narrative counseling,
　　7-8

Family therapy, 48, 96
Follow-up meetings, 87-88
Foucault, Michel, 21, 24
Frayling, Ian, ix

Gaze, the, 24-25, 123
Gender-based subject choices,
　dominant story of, 59
Gray-Yeates, Pamela, ix, 108
Groups/classes and communities,
　working with:
　appreciative audience to new
　　developments, 96
　class, working with a whole,
　　107-111
　communities of concern,
　　building, 100-103
　concentric pond ripples analogy,
　　97-98
　interviewing the problem, class-
　　room lessons built on, 111-114

"Journey, The" (adventure- based program), 104-107
narrative climate in the school, 117-119
school community, counselor alert to the unique aspects of a, 114-117
social fabric of stories, 95
wider audience to the new story, seeking out a, 98-100

Identity, constructing, 69, 98
Internalizing conversations, 38, 123
Interviewing the problem, classroom lessons built on, 111-114
Invitations to responsibility, 78
addressing violence or abuse, 79
examining misguided efforts, 81
respectful nonabusive ways of relating, 79-80
restraints, challenging, 84-86
time trends in behavior, identifying, 81 82

Jenkins, Alan, 78
Jordan, Elizabeth, ix
"Journey, The" (adventure-based program), 104-107

Knowledge, erosion of local, 63-64
Knowledge, respect for the client's, 29-30
Kottler, Jeffrey, ix

Landscape of meaning, 88
Length and the externalized problem, 39
Letters to clients, composing, 48
Lewis, Dorothea, ix
Lewis, Rolla, ix
Linguistic separation between the person and the problem, 41

Listening to problem-saturated story without getting stuck, 32-35, 37
Lived experience does not always get encapsulated in stories, 27
Local knowledge, erosion of, 63-64

Maori people, 23
Mapping-the-influence questions, 8-9, 39-43, 123
McKenzie, Wally, ix
McMenamin, Donald, ix
Meaning, the landscape of, 88
Medicalized descriptions, 61-62
Metaphor, narrative, 55-56
Methods, specific narrative:
assembling the alternative story, 44-47
caution, a, 49-50
documenting the evidence, 47
externalizing the problem, 35-40
listening to problem-saturated story without getting stuck, 32-35
Monk, Gerald, x
Monk, Heather-Ann, ix

Naming the problem with the client, sharing task of, 37-38
Narrative climate in the school, 117-119
Narrative metaphor, 55-56
Narrative therapy, vii-ix
See also individual subject headings
Narrative Therapy in Practice: The Archaeology of Hope (Winslade & Monk), x
Normality, describing, 59-60
Nuclear family, 96

Optimism, 28-29

Pakeha people, 23
Peripheral issues, avoid focusing
    on, 38
Persistence, 29
Personifications, developing
    externalizing descriptions
    into, 38-39
Pizzini, Nigel, ix
Postmodern thinking, narrative
    counseling founded in, 21, 123
Power of the teacher, 57-59
Power-sharing relationship,
    negotiating a, 30-31
Problematic talk, 52
Problems, people struggling with
    problems rather than being, 2
Problem-saturated stories,
    listening to, 32-35
Professionals, reliance on, 62-63
Publish archive of children's
    achievements, 48

Racism, 115-116
Reading list, 120-121
Re-authoring, 57, 71, 123
Redescription, process of, 65-66
Reflect upon and evaluate them-
    selves, student's ability to, 5
Reflection questions, 115
Relational skills, 32
Relationship with the client,
    establishing a strong, 5-6
Report forms asking teachers to
    notice performance of new
    story, 48
Reputations, reworking, 51
    deficit discourse, 59-64
    resistance, 64-66
    scenario, a narrative counseling,
        16-18
    schooling, the discourse of, 52-53
    teacher, the power of the, 57-59

Resistance to deficit-based
    descriptions, 64-66
Respect for people, 2, 28-29
Respectful behavior, restraints to,
    82-86
Responsibility. See Invitations to
    responsibility
Restraints to respectful behavior,
    82-86
Reversing internalizing logic of
    taken-for-granted discourses, 38

Scenario, a narrative counseling, 3
    alternative story, 11-13
    appreciative audience to new
        developments, 15-16
    background on student, 4
    competence and ability, client's
        areas of, 6, 10-11, 13-15
    curiosity, respectful, 6-7, 13
    documenting changes, 18-19
    externalizing conservation, 7-8
    mapping-the-influence
        questions, 8-9
    reflect upon and evaluate them-
        selves, student's ability to, 5
    relationship with the client,
        establishing a strong, 5-6
    reputation in a school, changing
        one's, 16-18
    unique outcomes, 9-10
Schooling, the discourse of, 52-53
    descriptions, school, 53-57
    narrative metaphor, 55-56
    re-authoring, 57
    school community, counselor
        alert to the unique aspects of
        a, 114-117
    See also Groups/classes and
        communities, working with
Scrutiny/surveillance, modern
    world characterized by norms
    kept in place by, 24-25

Self-description, 123
Self-enfeeblement, personal, 60-62
Sensitive topics, discussion of, 111-114
Significant others invited into counseling sessions, 47
Social control mechanisms supported by counseling, 71-72
Social fabric of stories, 95
Social marginalization, 69
Stealing trouble, 68-71
Stories, we live through, 2-3, 22
Stuart, Coral, ix
Surveillance/scrutiny, modern world characterized by norms kept in place by, 24-25
Suspensions, 116

Taking action, facilitate, 86-88
Teacher, the power of the, 57-59
Tentativeness, emphasis on a stance of, 30
Time trends in behavior, identifying, 81-82
Totalizing descriptions, 5-6, 70, 116, 123

Transformative change, 72
Trouble, conversations with kids who are in, 67-68
abusive behavior, combating, 77-89
classrooms, 71-76
disciplinary sense, counseling in a, 93-94
enrolling a new student, 92-93
stealing, 68-71
truancy, 89-92
Truancy trouble, 89-92

Unique aspects of a school community, counselor alert to the, 114-117
Unique outcomes, 9-10, 42, 44, 124

Vacuum, stories we live by are not produced in a, 22

Wagging (truancy), 89-92
White, Michael, vii, 21, 35
Who-the-hell-are-you tone, 74-75
Wider audience to the new story, seeking out a, 98-100
Winslade, John, x

CORWIN
PRESS

The Corwin Press logo—a raven striding across an open book—represents the happy union of courage and learning. We are a professional-level publisher of books and journals for K–12 educators, and we are committed to creating and providing resources that embody these qualities. Corwin's motto is "Success for All Learners."